AI FOR SCIENTIFIC DISCOVERY

AI for Scientific Discovery provides an accessible introduction to the wide-ranging applications of artificial intelligence (AI) technologies in scientific research and discovery across the full breadth of scientific disciplines. AI technologies support discovery science in multiple ways. They support literature management and synthesis, allowing the wealth of what has already been discovered and reported on to be integrated and easily accessed. They play a central role in data analysis and interpretation in the context of what is called 'data science'. AI is also helping to combat the reproducibility crisis in scientific research by underpinning the discovery process with AI-enabled standards and pipelines and supporting the management of large-scale data and knowledge resources so that they can be shared and integrated and serve as a background 'knowledge ecosystem' into which new discoveries can be embedded. However, there are limitations to what AI can achieve and its outputs can be biased and confounded and thus should not be blindly trusted. The latest generation of hybrid and 'human-in-the-loop' AI technologies have as their objective a balance between human inputs and insights and the power of number-crunching and statistical inference at a massive scale that AI technologies are best at.

AI FOR EVERYTHING SERIES

AI for Everything

Artificial intelligence (AI) is all around us. From driverless cars to game winning computers to fraud protection, AI is already involved in many aspects of life, and its impact will only continue to grow in future. Many of the world's most valuable companies are investing heavily in AI research and development, and not a day goes by without news of cutting-edge breakthroughs in AI and robotics.

The *AI for Everything* series explores the role of AI in contemporary life, from cars and aircraft to medicine, education, fashion and beyond. Concise and accessible, each book is written by an expert in the field and will bring the study and reality of AI to a broad readership including interested professionals, students, researchers, and lay readers.

AI for Death and Dying
Maggi Savin-Baden

AI for Creativity
Niklas Hageback

AI for Games
Ian Millington

AI for Sports
Chris Brady, Karl Tuyls, Shayegan Omidshafiei

AI for Learning
Carmel Kent & Benedict du Boulay

AI for the Sustainable Development Goals
Henrik Skaug Sætra

AI for School Teachers
Rose Luckin. Karine George & Mutlu Cukurova

AI for Healthcare Robotics
Eduard Fosch-Villaronga & Hadassah Drukarch

AI for Physics
Volker Knecht

AI for Diversity
Roger A. Søraa

AI for Finance
Edward P. K. Tsang

AI for Scientific Discovery
Janna Hastings

For more information about this series please visit:
https://www.routledge.com/AI-for-Everything/book-series/AIFE

AI FOR SCIENTIFIC DISCOVERY

JANNA HASTINGS

CRC Press
Taylor & Francis Group
Boca Raton London New York

CRC Press is an imprint of the
Taylor & Francis Group, an **informa** business

First edition published 2023
by CRC Press
6000 Broken Sound Parkway NW, Suite 300, Boca Raton, FL 33487-2742

and by CRC Press
4 Park Square, Milton Park, Abingdon, Oxon, OX14 4RN

CRC Press is an imprint of Taylor & Francis Group, LLC

ISBN: 978-1-032-12877-1 (hbk)
ISBN: 978-1-032-12484-1 (pbk)
ISBN: 978-1-003-22664-2 (ebk)

DOI: 10.1201/9781003226642

Typeset in Joanna
by KnowledgeWorks Global Ltd.

CONTENTS

PREFACE

This text is about artificial intelligence (AI) in its many different forms and about scientific discovery across a wide range of disciplines. It has grown out of my years of working precisely in the borderlands between scientific research and digital technology and of observing the interactions between scientists and the information systems that are developed with the objective of (even if they do not always succeed in) making scientific research easier and more automated.

The text has been influenced by many different projects I have worked on. I have drawn extensively from experiences gained in the context of the Human Behaviour-Change Project, an ambitious project that aims to use AI to automate evidence synthesis in the behavioural sciences. I have also drawn from my PhD research into the metabolic changes that take place during ageing, which used 'big data' and computational mathematical simulations, and from my postdoctoral work in a neuroscience laboratory. Finally, the text draws from my experience working closely together with scientists during the many years I have been a scientific ontologist, which is a little-known but essential role in modern scientific research that involves capturing and standardising the entities that scientific investigations are about in a form that computers can use and reason over. Trying to 'teach' human knowledge to computers forces one to be clearer about what it is that we know or need to communicate about, and perhaps thereby to confront a little more directly the nature of the world itself. And, when trying to do this in a standardised way so that the effort has a unifying impact on a research discipline, one is forced to confront the social processes involved in scientific research, the ever-present human dimension behind the scenes of the shiny pages on which discoveries are reported.

In my career, I have alternated between *doing* scientific discovery, that is, seeing discovery from the lens of the scientific process, the research questions themselves and the effort in trying to answer them, and then *making use of* scientific discoveries as a resource, that is, seeing scientific discovery from the lens of the research outputs as entities which need to be processed, captured, exchanged and integrated. I have benefited from an outsider perspective at times, and an insider perspective at other times, for different disciplines and communities, in different projects with different aims and objectives. Yet a common theme throughout all my experiences of modern scientific research environments is that digital technology and its evolution are becoming inescapably intertwined with the scientific questions that we are asking and seeking to answer, just as digital technology is being intertwined with our personal and political lives, and the conversations we are having with each other and in the media across the divides of cultures and languages and borders. And as digital technology is given more and more power to influence choices and have an influence on our lives, in science and in culture alike, it becomes more important to take a closer look at the nature of the technology itself, not only to herald its potential but also to be honest about its capabilities and its limitations.

To make our digital technologies work better for people, we need to better understand those people, and listen to them, which in the case of scientific discovery is the scientists themselves. We need to observe them in their interactions with their digital systems. And we need to seek carefully to understand where the gaps are between what we could achieve and what we currently have, between what the scientists expect and hope for from their digital support tools, and what indeed those systems do or could offer. This exploration intrinsically requires interdisciplinarity, shifting between perspectives. And it requires a shared passion for the outcome, which in this case is scientific discovery itself.

ACKNOWLEDGEMENTS

I am enormously grateful to Robert West, Susan Michie, Fabian Neuhaus, Martin Glauer, Till Mossakowski, Christian Lovis, Barry Smith, Stefan Schulz, Christoph Steinbeck, my colleagues and collaborators in the Centre for Behaviour Change at University College London, and my colleagues at the Institute for Intelligent Interacting Systems at the Otto-von-Guericke University in Magdeburg, for the many interesting and inspiring discussions about scientific research and digital technology that have informed the ideas contained in this text.

Some of these ideas were presented in preliminary form at the workshop *Qurator: Digital Curation* held virtually from Berlin in February 2021, at the workshop *AI 4 Scientific Discovery* held in Southampton in March 2022, at the *Medical Informatics in Europe* conference held in Nice in May 2022 and at the workshop *To trust or not to trust: When should AI be allowed to make decisions?* held in Lausanne in September 2022.

I am also particularly grateful to Robert West, Jeremy Frey and Barry Smith for providing very helpful feedback on an earlier draft of this text. Despite all these positive influences, all errors and shortcomings that remain in the text are solely the responsibility of the author.

ABOUT THE AUTHOR

Janna Hastings is a computer scientist with more than a decade of experience across the life, behavioural and social sciences. She is also a data scientist with a PhD in computational biology and extensive experience in bioinformatics, cheminformatics and psychoinformatics. She is currently Assistant Professor of Medical Knowledge and Decision Support at the University of Zurich, and Vice-Director of the School of Medicine at the University of St. Gallen. Her current research focuses on bridging the gaps between knowledge and learning to bring AI technologies in medicine closer to the needs and workflows of clinicians and to support truly interdisciplinary and integrative knowledge discovery.

1

INTRODUCTION

AI AND THE DIGITAL
REVOLUTION IN SCIENCE

Few ideas have captured the popular imagination of our era as much as that of artificial intelligence – a vision of intelligent machines able to act and think as humans do. The promises and perils of potentially intelligent machines are constantly being imagined, presented, debated and reframed across all media and information channels. Some of these visions are purely fantastical: we are very far from needing to be concerned that robot superhumans may be about to take over the world or to put all humans out of work in our lifetimes. However, artificial intelligence technologies – in the real-world sense of what this means in practice, about which I will elaborate shortly – nevertheless are making inroads in many areas of human life. Nearly every week, a headline proclaims a new breakthrough for artificial intelligence technology – whether it is winning at sophisticated card games, steering self-driving cars, predicting how proteins will fold or explaining jokes, artificial intelligence technology appears to be overcoming challenges on all frontiers. The hope for artificial intelligence technologies is that they will enable us to automate, speed up and scale up all human activities in a way that will allow us to be freed from boring, tedious or challenging tasks,

DOI: 10.1201/9781003226642-1

while simultaneously accelerating the pace of progress on all frontiers, not least of all that of scientific discovery – that scientists might
be entirely freed from drudgery and repetition, while an army of
machines buzzes around in laboratories, shifting and mixing materials, constructing, steering, filtering and suggesting interpretations,
in an ever-accelerating race to the discoveries that stand to change
the world.

SCIENTIFIC DISCOVERY

WHAT IS SCIENTIFIC DISCOVERY?

Few hallmarks of the modern era are more tangible and concrete
than the steady march of scientific innovation and the accompanying technological advancement. Across a wide range of different
disciplines, scientific questions are answered through an astonish-
ingly diverse collection of methods and analytic practices, with a
tiny selection of the discoveries in the last century spanning from
Einstein's general theory of relativity to the mapping of the human
genome, the development of novel vaccination technologies to
combat the SARS-CoV-2 virus, advances in the understanding of
the complex relationships between socioeconomic conditions and
life outcomes and increasingly accurate predictions of the effects of
human activities on the global climate. Scientific discoveries under-
pin the advancement of standards of living across the developed
world and are at the forefront of hopes and objectives for continued
global development into the future.

Scientific discovery has been defined as 'the process or product
of successful scientific inquiry' (Schickore, 2018). It is difficult to
pin down exactly what scientific discovery means, as this may vary
in theory and in practice for different types of questions, different sorts of entities, different domains and different methodological
approaches. Different disciplinary specialisations, such as physics,
psychology, chemistry, biology and medicine, have evolved an abun-
dance of methods and practices for robustly, reliably and efficiently

discovering more about all aspects of the world that fall within their scope of interest and applicability.

One dimension of scientific discovery is that of *novelty*, that is, *discovery* involves finding out something that was not known before or creating something of a type that did not exist before. Some examples include new ways of manufacturing stronger and lighter materials (Zeng *et al.*, 2022), the discovery of new types of exotic matter (Castelvecchi, 2021) and the discovery of evidence that humans were using tobacco 12,300 years ago, 9,000 years earlier than had previously been thought to be the earliest tobacco use (Duke *et al.*, 2022).

Another dimension of scientific discovery is that of it being *scientific*, and although the precise nuances of what that means or how it should be defined have been the subject of extensive debate (Kampourakis, 2016), a typical dictionary definition offers the somewhat circular proposal that it is 'based on or characterised by the methods and principles of science'. This suggests that in order to better understand what it means to be scientific, we should start with what the scientific method is and what scientific principles are.

The scientific method can be described as an information flow-driven active process in which evidence gives rise to questions that in turn lead to theories and hypotheses, that are then tested through experiments, that in turn lead to data, that in turn lead to interpretations and new findings and that then in turn give rise to further evidence and inform further questions (Figure 1.1).

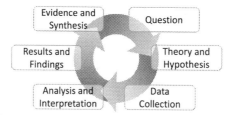

Figure 1.1 The scientific method conceptualised as a cyclic directed process.

In practice, back and forth between the steps may occur at any stage, many different variations of the theme of scientific discovery take place depending on the exact nature of the scientific question about which discoveries are being made, and there is also a proven role for chance or luck (Gaughan, 2010). Scientific discovery advances cumulatively through the aggregate activities of scientific research, which encompass many deliberate processes of synthesis, testing and reporting with the objective of generating new insights into, and accumulating knowledge about, the world and everything in it. And, scientific research makes up a significant portion of the economy in developed countries (Macilwain, 2010), benefiting from both governmental and nongovernmental investments.

TECHNOLOGY AND DIGITALISATION IN SCIENTIFIC DISCOVERY

Technology is important to the advance of scientific research in many different ways. Across many disciplines, the sorts of questions that scientists ask can often only be answered through the development of technologies that are able to help us to gather the data that would let us answer those questions. For example, technology often mediates measurement and observation: we cannot observe individual virus particles directly with our eyes, but we can do so through powerful microscopes; neither can we observe the gamma-ray radiation generated by the distant collisions of immense celestial bodies with our eyes, but we can record it through powerful telescopes. Technology sometimes allows us to perform experiments that we would not otherwise be able to perform – for example, in order to test the prediction of Einstein's special theory of relativity that time would speed up or slow down under acceleration, atomic clocks were flown at high speed around the world and indeed were observed to have slowed down or sped up in keeping with the theory's predictions (Hafele and Keating, 1972). Often, technological advances allow our investigations to be larger and more comprehensive than they would otherwise have been.

Increasingly, scientific research, along with many other domains, is becoming *digitised*, that is, it is becoming supported by and performed by means of information − digital − technologies, in a pervasive change in working practices throughout the modern world known as *digital transformation*. Digital transformation is being hailed as a paradigm shift in how research is conducted across the full range of different scientific domains, for example, in the development of new materials (Kimmig, Zechel and Schubert, 2021), in medicine (Berisha *et al.*, 2021), including mental health (Bucci, Schwannauer and Berry, 2019; Hastings, 2020), and in behavioural science (Hesse, 2020). Digital transformation is, of course, also affecting the world outside of scientific research − in the developed world, our lives and our work are increasingly digitalised. The pace at which information technology has been developed and has pervasively impacted our ways of working across different sectors and aspects of life has been breathtaking, leading some to call these developments a revolution on a par with the industrial revolution − a comprehensive change in the way that we live, work and interconnect with each other.

In many ways, digital transformation means *more* − for example, we consume more information, more rapidly, with a wider geographic reach. Science is no exception. For scientific research, digital technology also means *more*: more projects involving bigger teams, bigger experiments leading to more data and more published results in more published scientific reports in an ever-increasing diversity of publication outlets. Information technology is pervasively transforming scientific measurement, data analyses and interpretation, the publication of scientific findings and the process of finding and synthesising existing research.

And among all the digital technologies, one of those with the largest potential for impacting our ways of conducting scientific research is artificial intelligence: the promise of automated systems that are able to assist scientific investigations by performing tasks at a level that parallels that of humans.

ARTIFICIAL INTELLIGENCE

WHAT IS ARTIFICIAL INTELLIGENCE?

Any sufficiently advanced technology is indistinguishable from magic

(CLARKE, 1968)

Artificial intelligence is certainly imbued in the popular eye with an aura of magic in precisely the sense reflected in Arthur C. Clarke's famous 'third law', quoted above. Clarke was writing about the difficulty in predicting what is possible and what is impossible and the way that technologies of the future tend to break through the barriers set for them by the imagination of even the best scientists of a given time, giving breakthroughs of technologies the appearance of magic when viewed through the lens of any era that has passed. However, both in the case of technologies in general and artificial intelligence in particular this can be a double-edged sword that works both ways. Sometimes, our predictions for the future are truly magical, in the sense that the technologies they would require not only do not exist yet but also in principle cannot exist. Moreover, there is a sense in which we do not usually regard something as magical if we know how it works, that is, if we know that it is a commonplace technology. The idea of artificial intelligence is itself an idea infused with magic, but with the corollary that we often don't regard digital automated systems as 'artificial intelligence' if we know how they work. There is a risk, then, that each new innovation in digital technology in support of automated reasoning, learning and action is initially seen as artificial intelligence but then thereafter, as it becomes accepted and pervasive, transitions into the background and is just called rules or inference or machine learning, depending on how it works. Thereby, the label 'artificial intelligence' is continuously able to preserve its mystique, but at the cost of presenting an everchanging and shifting target. We should be wary of this tendency and mindful of the fact that not every digital technology for which we do not understand how it works is necessarily intelligent, and neither is everything we do understand not intelligent. In considering what 'artificial intelligence' means in practice, we should also be mindful of the extent to which digital technologies are or are not truly artificial, in the sense that they are supported by inputs and algorithms crafted carefully by humans. And finally, we should be mindful that the concept of intelligence itself can be, even in humans, a slippery and shifting idea to pin down.

What it means to be intelligent, and how intelligence relates to other human aptitudes and capabilities, has been debated and contested throughout the last century (Sternberg, 2019). Some researchers consider there to be just one general dimension of intelligence across all domains and tasks, while others consider different domains, skills and aptitudes as separate dimensions. It is impossible to come up with an exhaustive list of what intelligence consists of, but it is usually considered to include at least the central human abilities such as understanding the world and specific contexts, communicating through the use of language and symbols, reasoning and inference, planning and executing effective actions to bring about the realisation of one's goals, self-awareness, motivation, learning, the ability to perceive information and develop models and abstractions which can be logically manipulated through critical thinking, creativity and problem-solving. More generally, we could describe intelligence as the generalised ability to adapt and act appropriately, given a particular environment or context – even when that context has never been previously encountered. And for scientific discovery, it is important not to overlook the importance of creativity – many new discoveries were a direct result of thinking outside the narrow confines of what had been thought before, making connections between previously unconnected entities.

Artificial intelligence can be defined in several different ways (Russell, Norvig and Davis, 2010; Marcus, 2020; Landgrebe and Smith, 2022), which vary in the extent to which they rely on the dimensions of what machines are able to do or how they are able to do it. The most common definitions in current use refer to the ability to *perform tasks* that would require intelligence if performed by humans. The 'Turing Test', proposed by the British mathematician and early pioneer of artificial intelligence Alan Turing, provides an example of such a definition of artificially intelligent systems. To pass the Turing Test, a human being should be unable to distinguish an artificially intelligent system from another human using the replies to questions put to both. Intuitively, this makes sense, as what indicates intelligence better than behaviour, such as conversational replies, being indistinguishable from that of humans? However, it can, of course, be objected that this definition allows for processes that appear to be intelligent but nevertheless are not, in that they do not, in fact, perform those tasks *in an intelligent way*.

This distinction matters if one is interested in genuine, and general, intelligence of the sort that humans have. Some have claimed that the trajectory of the development of artificially intelligent technologies will soon lead them to possess capabilities beyond even those of humans, to become 'superhuman' (e.g., Bostrom, 2017). It is easy to see why such claims have captured the public imagination, whether as visions of a utopian future or fears of a dystopian age of human subservience to super-intelligent non-human masters. However, despite the headlines, the technologies we do have access to are extremely far from realising *general* (or genuine) artificial intelligence (and there are those who have argued that they will never be able to achieve this, e.g., Marcus, 2018; Landgrebe and Smith, 2022). Rather, the systems that are called artificially intelligent today are tailor-made for specific direct tasks and specific well-defined challenges, that is, they are narrow in their scope rather than broad or general. Moreover, it can be debated whether what they do reflects intelligence in any meaningful sense except perhaps the sense in which they 'reflect' the human intelligence used to design them and to generate the data that they learn from. Nevertheless, they do satisfy the definition that they perform tasks that would require intelligence in humans to perform, and they do so in an expanding range of applications for which they are already proving very useful. To have a better sense of what artificial intelligence can and cannot do, it may be useful to know something about the different types of artificial intelligence technologies that exist today and the different challenges they address.

TYPES OF ARTIFICIAL INTELLIGENCE

There are many different types of artificial intelligence technologies designed to solve different challenges (Figure 1.2). These are broadly grouped into three areas:

1. Technologies that support machine learning – processes that involve training with some input data and example outputs, to learn to make a prediction of an output given similar inputs.
2. Technologies that support reasoning – that is, given some facts and axioms, being able to deduce the logical consequences of those facts and axioms or find logical inconsistencies.
3. Technologies that support behaving in the world – that is, sensing the environment and being able to interact with the environment in some way.

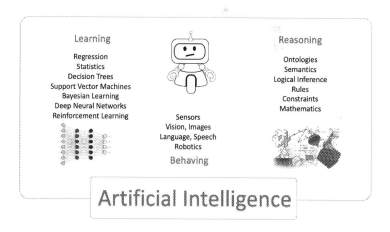

Figure 1.2 Types of artificial intelligence technology grouped by their objective.

Of course, any of these different technologies can be used in combination with each other, and most of the more sophisticated applications require multiple of these components.

Many of the most recent breakthroughs in artificial intelligence across domains, including scientific discovery, have arisen from a particular type of artificial intelligence technology which would more technically be known as machine learning in the form of 'deep' neural networks. These systems, designed to emulate information flowing between neurons in the brain, consist of large numbers of artificial 'neurons' that are connected together in 'layers' and involve complex mathematical functions which pass information from one layer to the next (and back again) in order to arrive at an optimal state to perform a given behaviour that involves transforming inputs into the desired output. It is worth observing that despite the name, the 'neurons' in artificial neural networks do not really resemble the neurons in a human brain, except in the most abstract sense of being information processing units that take in inputs and provide outputs. Nor do the simplified layered architectures of artificial neural networks reflect the densely interconnected and sophisticated architecture of the human brain with its different tissues, cell types, functional modules and overarching density of information processing.

DEEP NEURAL NETWORKS

The 'deep' in the expression 'deep neural network' refers to the number of layers such a network has between the direct input-processing layer and the output layer, which are called 'hidden' layers: while the illustration (bottom left of Figure 1.2) shows just two such layers, typically such networks can be much larger, encompassing ten or even a hundred such layers. Each node (or artificial 'neuron') in the network takes multiple inputs from other nodes in the network and transforms them to produce output by using a learned mathematical function that has many parameters. These parameters are 'trained' in a process that involves feeding the network with input data and examples of the correct output expected for that input and then 'backpropagating' information about incorrect predictions from the output layer back to the hidden layers in order to adjust the parameter values.

Each layer in the network adds the possibility to learn more subtle distinctions between inputs and thereby make more nuanced and accurate predictions of outputs. As a result, considering all the nodes and layers, this type of network learns an overall function with a vast number of parameters – each node and connection in the network has its own parameters. The training process which sets the parameter values typically uses a mathematical optimisation algorithm that is able to efficiently (given enough computing power) detect the configuration that gives rise to the most successful prediction output for the specified training data. Because there are so many parameters that have to be set for the network to be able to make good predictions, deep neural networks are only feasible when there are large quantities of training data available to use for training the internal state of the network, and in part, the rapid proliferation of their successes in recent years reflects the wider availability of large-scale data as much as it does improved architectures.

Deep neural networks are not a single, but rather a whole family of approaches: many different architectures and mathematical functions for this type of learning system have been developed, and new ones are being developed all the time. Due to the successes of these networks in overcoming previously unsolved challenges, research into deep neural network architectures is prolific. Novel elements are regularly added to such frameworks and where such elements bring a significant improvement in the state of the art, those architectures tend to become the more commonly used. For example, just a few years ago a mechanism was introduced that allowed for a selective 'attention' state to be maintained at each layer of a deep neural network, allowing nodes in a network to selectively adjust the importance they place on different parts of the overall input when computing the output, in addition to the other parameters each node maintains (Vaswani *et al.*, 2017). Since then, networks using attention mechanisms have become very widely used and outperform earlier approaches for a multitude of applications.

The purposes to which artificial neural networks have been applied are diverse: tasks include recommending what to buy based on purchase history as is done by online retailers such as Amazon, detecting objects in images in order to categorise the images based on what they depict, translating from one language to another automatically, suggesting disease diagnoses from medical observations such as chest x-rays and, of course, interpreting the results of scientific experiments. Their performance for many tasks has been impressive. We can see the utility of such computations in the many examples of artificial intelligence applications that we interact with on a regular basis, such as search engines that suggest corrections to mistyped search queries. However, deep neural networks nevertheless only manifest one aspect of (narrow) intelligence, which is based on the ability to learn patterns from large-scale data and to compute similarities. Such networks cannot perform general goal-directed logical reasoning or planning, they do not exhibit common sense or explicit awareness of their environments, nor can they typically solve problems outside the domain that they have been trained for. Moreover, they tend to reflect the features and problems inherent in the data they are trained on, which can lead to biases and problems in their behaviour. For example, inherent statistical biases plague the automated translations of natural language texts using this type of technology. For example, the English 'they' is translated into the masculine 'ils' in French, even when the 'they' in question happen to be giving birth – an example of a context that would clearly indicate translation into the female form would be more appropriate – because 'they' has no gender in English, and the more masculine form is more common in French texts (Savoldi *et al.*, 2021). As another example of gender bias, networks that are trained to suggest characteristic images for labels may suggest exclusively male images for the prompt 'doctor' but exclusively female for the prompt 'assistant', reflecting biases in the data available for training.

SYMBOLIC ARTIFICIAL INTELLIGENCE

Aside from neural networks, there are other forms of artificial intelligence that have different foundations, giving rise to different strengths and weaknesses. A technology that is sometimes called 'good old-fashioned artificial intelligence' because it was one of the first approaches to be developed in the early days of artificial intelligence research involves the use of systems of symbols to represent facts about things in the world and systems of inference based on logical rules that are able to deduce implicit consequences from the knowledge that is thereby expressed. For example, if we have represented that *all men do yoga* and *Frank is a man*, then we can infer that *Frank does yoga*. There are many different formalisms for representing this type of explicit knowledge and for deriving inferences from it, ranging from simple approaches that are only able to represent basic logical propositions to complex systems that are able to integrate logic, rules and mathematics. Such systems are called 'expert' systems because they are designed to recapitulate the knowledge and inferences of human experts in a given domain. One of the first artificial intelligence-based expert systems, developed nearly 60 years ago at Stanford, DENDRAL (short for Dendritic Algorithm; Lederberg, 1987; Lindsay *et al.*, 1993), was designed to conduct scientific reasoning in the chemical domain – to determine the overall structure of molecules based on information about the parts. Incidentally, this problem is one for which artificial intelligence is still widely applied today (e.g., Howarth, Ermanis and Goodman, 2020).

Neural networks are only able to learn *implicit* knowledge: their complex connectivity structures and message-passing weights that have been learned during training are only accessible in use when the network is applied to the task. The network is able to act on an input to produce an output but is not able to explain on what basis the output is produced in terms of the input. In contrast, knowledge-based systems are constructed from explicit knowledge that can be explored, interacted with and directly updated and queried, which makes such systems much more transparent.

Knowledge-based systems are also still in regular use today, and their technologies are similarly evolving to be more powerful and address a wider range of tasks. Most modern platforms that offer intelligent behaviour, such as search or recommendation systems, use some combination of neural networks and explicit knowledge-based systems behind the scenes. Moreover, approaches to building 'hybrid' systems that harness the best of both of these types of artificial intelligence architectures are one of the main frontiers of current technological research in artificial intelligence (Alshahrani et al., 2017; Garcez and Lamb, 2020).

But to come back to the topic at hand, we might ask: what intelligent processes are involved in scientific discovery? And which of these are amenable to being automated or augmented with artificial intelligence?

ARTIFICIAL INTELLIGENCE FOR SCIENTIFIC DISCOVERY

Each of the steps involved in scientific discovery is at least potentially a target for the development of a supporting artificial intelligence solution. The topic of artificial intelligence for scientific discovery is immense in scope, and it is of course therefore impossible to produce a comprehensive survey of the topic. This text aims to be indicative rather than comprehensive, to illustrate rather than to systematically map. Thus, it only includes selective, biased coverage of some recent advances of note, aiming to give just an idea of the possibilities with their transformative potential as well as the associated challenges.

Arguably, scientific discovery in the modern research context begins and ends with scientific reports or publications. A more traditional view of the scientific discovery process would begin with a hypothesis and end once some evidence has shown support for or against the hypothesis; however, in the modern era, scientific research processes are heavily embedded in publication practices. The discovery process begins with publications because all discoveries build on earlier work, which must first be explored, understood and integrated, before the opportunities for new (publishable) discoveries and research directions can be determined. And it ends with publications because after a study has been conducted, it needs to be reported in order to be disseminated to the scientific community. Thus, one of the most important applications of artificial intelligence technologies to scientific discovery is in facilitating and automating (to the extent possible) the management and processing of the enormous body of scientific publications that constitute the literature in any given domain, and this is the subject of *Chapter 2 – AI for managing scientific literature and evidence*. There are many parts of the overall scientific literature management process which are difficult and slow to do manually – and may even be impossible to do comprehensively due to the rate at which the literature grows – but which are being significantly enhanced by the application of a family of artificial intelligence technologies known as natural language processing. For example, for any given research question, *relevant* research has to be sifted out of the huge volumes of other research in tangential domains. This involves the automated processing of huge collections of titles and abstracts and classifying them as relevant or not. Once relevant research has been identified, specific information needs to be extracted from that research, for example, we may be interested in identifying individual drugs that are mentioned together with the diseases they may treat or side effects that they may cause. Beyond identifying mentions of things we are interested in, to be optimally effective as a 'robot' research assistant, an artificial intelligence system would be able to identify automatically from a scientific publication what scientific question was being addressed by the research, what the experimental design was, what the data indicated and what the researchers have concluded was the outcome. This level of interconnected and contextual processing of a scientific report is still out of reach for the technologies in use today but constitutes an exciting research frontier for artificial intelligence technologies in the future.

Another area in which scientific discovery is benefiting from artificial intelligence is in the interpretation of data, the subject of *Chapter 3 – AI for data interpretation*. The adequate interpretation of data in a context typically requires quantitative approaches to be applied in combination with theoretical frameworks and background knowledge. Intelligence is involved in selecting the appropriate theoretical background to frame a particular question, designing a study and data collection to answer the question and interpreting the resulting dataset to answer the question. Across many disciplines, increasingly, with advancing automation and data measurement technologies, we are witnessing an explosion of the size of data available with which to answer questions – a phenomenon often referred to as 'big data'. The scale of the data in the thousands to millions of data points (or more) prevents traditional approaches for data analysis and interpretation from being effective; thus, new approaches are being developed that can search for meaning and patterns in complex, noisy data. An advanced frontier for artificial intelligence in data analysis and interpretation for scientific discovery would be for artificially intelligent systems to be able not only to interpret results to answer specific questions but also to generate appropriate questions – and select appropriate theoretical frameworks in which to do so. A crucial component of intelligence driving this aspect of scientific discovery is the ability to think and reason causally. Moreover, the ability to determine meaningful, ethical and important research questions is a nuance that requires a wider awareness of the background within which scientific discovery leads to advances in the frontiers of knowledge, which is not always obvious even for humans to understand. Sometimes, scientific questions become irrelevant due to paradigm shifts in the foundational understanding of the domain.

Aside from the knowledge-oriented aspects of scientific discovery, there are also practical aspects – designing and conducting experiments, and ensuring experiments can be repeated. This is the focus of *Chapter 4: AI for reproducible research*. Designing experiments involves planning, the automation of which involves a different form of artificial intelligence than that required in data interpretation or natural language processing. Planning involves the construction and optimisation of sequences of actions, each of which takes the outputs from the previous step as inputs and applies a transformation to generate a new set of outputs. A common artificial intelligence technique used in experimental design is called active learning – where a system is trained to generate possible steps to get closer to some specified objective and is able to iteratively reduce uncertainty in a combinatorial search space by suggesting targeted experiments that might be performed to gather information. Moreover, for many areas of scientific discovery, the driving force enabling the advance of science is technological automation such as robotic or mechanical devices that are controlled by artificial intelligence. Advancing automation of this sort frees humans from the need to do mechanical and repetitive tasks, while simultaneously expanding the scope of what can be done both in scale and in type.

Artificial intelligence offers many opportunities for advancing scientific discovery. However, there are also challenges with the application of artificial intelligence technologies in their current form. Limitations, ethics, trust and how they play out in artificial intelligence for science are the subjects of *Chapter 5 – Limitations of AI and strategies for combating bias*. These include limitations of the technologies and the gaps that at present we do not know how to overcome as well as biases that are learned from data and those that are inherent in the algorithms themselves. Legal regulations are being implemented in many countries and regions to address these challenges and ensure that artificial intelligence technologies are developed and used responsibly, and many such regulations require a certain amount of transparency in the algorithms, which is known as interpretability. To ultimately succeed in transforming scientific discovery, artificial intelligence technology will need to be trusted by the humans who use it, and for this to happen, the technologies will need to be ethical and trustworthy. This is by no means guaranteed by the algorithms but needs to be built in explicitly.

Despite the limitations, artificial intelligence technologies are already making an impact in every aspect of scientific discovery, and this trend is likely to continue. What does a vision for artificial intelligence-involving science look like? This is the subject of *Chapter 6 – AI and the future of scientific discovery*. While the trend of increasing acceleration and increasing automation is of course likely to continue, this chapter looks at frontiers that have the potential to make a step change over and above the pace of steady progress. These will involve systems that can learn continuously, keep themselves up to date and drive creative innovation. It will also involve systems that have an explicit understanding of the subject matter of each domain and how those domains are inter-related, allowing translations and synthesis to cross historical disciplinary boundaries and accelerate innovation on a wider, more integrated discovery frontier for each different question. It may not be the case that genuine intelligence is within reach for artificially intelligent systems. Nevertheless, the increasing development of such systems is likely to give rise to a new sense of partnership between humans and technological systems which ultimately frees humans up to better focus on what matters most to them, and by so doing enhances not only scientific discovery but also the quality of life for scientists and non-scientists alike.

REFERENCES

Alshahrani, M. *et al.* (2017) 'Neuro-symbolic representation learning on biological knowledge graphs', *Bioinformatics*, 33(17), pp. 2723–2730. Available at: https://doi.org/10.1093/bioinformatics/btx275.

Berisha, V. *et al.* (2021) 'Digital medicine and the curse of dimensionality', *npj Digital Medicine*, 4(1), pp. 1–8. Available at: https://doi.org/10.1038/s41746-021-00521-5.

Bostrom, N. (2017) Superintelligence. Oxford: Oxford University Press.

Bucci, S., Schwannauer, M. and Berry, N. (2019) 'The digital revolution and its impact on mental health care', *Psychology and Psychotherapy*, 92(2), pp. 277–297. Available at: https://doi.org/10.1111/papt.12222.

Castelvecchi, D. (2021) 'Exotic four-quark particle spotted at Large Hadron Collider', *Nature*, 596(7872), pp. 330–330. Available at: https://doi.org/10.1038/d41586-021-02174-6.

Clarke, A.C. (1968) 'Clarke's Third Law on UFO's', *Science*, 159(3812), pp. 255–255. Available at: https://doi.org/10.1126/science.159.3812.255.c.

Duke, D. *et al.* (2022) 'Earliest evidence for human use of tobacco in the Pleistocene Americas', *Nature Human Behaviour*, 6(2), pp. 183–192. Available at: https://doi.org/10.1038/s41562-021-01202-9.

Garcez, A. d'Avila and Lamb, L.C. (2020) 'Neurosymbolic AI: The 3rd wave', *arXiv:2012.05876* [cs] [Preprint]. Available at: http://arxiv.org/abs/2012.05876 (Accessed: 5 September 2021).

Gaughan, R. (2010) *Accidental Genius*. New York : Metro Books. Available at: http://archive.org/details/accidentalgenius0000gaug_t4k9 (Accessed: 10 October 2022).

Hafele, C. and Keating, R.E. (1972) 'Around-the-world atomic clocks: Predicted relativistic time gains', *Science*, 177(4044), pp. 166–168.

Hastings, J. (2020) *Mental Health Ontologies: How We Talk about Mental Health, and Why It Matters in the Digital Age*. Exeter: University of Exeter Press.

Hesse, B.W. (2020) 'Riding the wave of digital transformation in behavioral medicine', *Annals of Behavioral Medicine: A Publication of the Society of Behavioral Medicine*, 54(12), pp. 960–967. Available at: https://doi.org/10.1093/abm/kaaa093.

Howarth, A., Ermanis, K. and Goodman, J.M. (2020) 'DP4-AI automated NMR data analysis: Straight from spectrometer to structure', *Chemical Science*, 11(17), pp. 4351–4359. Available at: https://doi.org/10.1039/D0SC00442A.

Kampourakis, K. (2016) '(The) nature(s) of science(s) and (the) scientific method(s)', *Science & Education*, 25(1), pp. 1–2. Available at: https://doi.org/10.1007/s11191-016-9804-z.

Kimmig, J., Zechel, S. and Schubert, U.S. (2021) 'Digital transformation in materials science: A paradigm change in material's development', *Advanced Materials (Deerfield Beach, Fla.)*, 33(8), p. e2004940. Available at: https://doi.org/10.1002/adma.202004940.

Landgrebe, J. and Smith, B. (2022) *Why Machines Will Never Rule the Earth: AI without Fear*. New York, NY: Routledge.

Lederberg, J. (1987) 'How DENDRAL Was Conceived and Born', in *Proceedings of ACM Conference on History of Medical Informatics*. New York, NY: Association for Computing Machinery (HMI '87), pp. 5–19. Available at: https://doi.org/10.1145/41526.41528.

Lindsay, R.K. *et al.* (1993) 'DENDRAL: A case study of the first expert system for scientific hypothesis formation', *Artificial Intelligence*, 61(2), pp. 209–261. Available at: https://doi.org/10.1016/0004-3702(93)90068-M.

Macilwain, C. (2010) 'Science economics: What science is really worth', *Nature*, 465(7299), pp. 682–684. Available at: https://doi.org/10.1038/465682a.

Marcus, G. (2018) 'Deep learning: A critical appraisal'. arXiv. Available at: https://doi.org/10.48550/arXiv.1801.00631.

Marcus, G. (2020) 'The next decade in AI: Four steps towards robust artificial intelligence'. Available at: https://arxiv.org/vc/arxiv/papers/2002/2002.06177v1.pdf.

Russell, S.J., Norvig, P. and Davis, E. (2010) *Artificial Intelligence: A Modern Approach*. 3rd ed. Upper Saddle River, NJ: Prentice Hall (Prentice Hall series in artificial intelligence).

Savoldi, B. *et al.* (2021) 'Gender bias in machine translation', *Transactions of the Association for Computational Linguistics*, 9, pp. 845–874. Available at: https://doi.org/10.1162/tacl_a_00401.

Schickore, J. (2018) 'Scientific Discovery', in E.N. Zalta (ed.) *The Stanford Encyclopedia of Philosophy*. Summer. Metaphysics Research Lab, Stanford University. Available at: https://plato.stanford.edu/archives/sum2018/entries/scientific-discovery/ (Accessed: 13 April 2022).

Sternberg, R.J. (2019) 'A theory of adaptive intelligence and its relation to general intelligence', *Journal of Intelligence*, 7(4), p. E23. Available at: https://doi.org/10.3390/jintelligence7040023.

Vaswani, A. *et al.* (2017) 'Attention is all you need', *arXiv:1706.03762 [cs]* [Preprint]. Available at: http://arxiv.org/abs/1706.03762 (Accessed: 6 October 2020).

Zeng, Y. *et al.* (2022) 'Irreversible synthesis of an ultrastrong two-dimensional polymeric material', *Nature*, 602(7895), pp. 91–95. Available at: https://doi.org/10.1038/s41586-021-04296-3.

2

AI FOR MANAGING SCIENTIFIC LITERATURE AND EVIDENCE

We are drowning in information but starved for knowledge.

(JOHN NAISBITT)

It has been claimed, famously, that *"science would not exist, if scientific results are not communicated"* (van Raan, 2004). Although it is not the only output of scientific discovery, a very important output in the modern research context is the scientific publication, the report in which scientific work and scientific findings are communicated to the broader scientific community and to the public.

As discussed in the previous chapter, an important element of scientific discovery is that what is discovered is novel, or at least, presents novel evidence that increases confidence in a previous discovery. One of the biggest challenges facing modern-day scientists is how to keep up to date with the research that is ongoing in every aspect of their subject matter and discipline in order to determine what has already been discovered and to continuously survey the landscape of evolving scientific knowledge. Thousands of new scientific publications in the form of books, reports and journal articles are published in each discipline every day. Scientific activity across every discipline is growing exponentially (Larsen and von Ins, 2010), both in pace and in output, with an estimated doubling

DOI: 10.1201/9781003226642-2

Figure 2.1   A search for 'COVID-19' in the popular biomedical literature database PubMed yields more than 305,000 journal articles in late 2022.

time of around 17 years on average (Bornmann and Mutz, 2015; Bornmann, Haunschild and Mutz, 2021).

For example, more than 305,000 journal articles relating to COVID have been indexed in the popular biomedical literature database PubMed (pubmed.ncbi.nlm.nih.gov) from the start of the pandemic until the time of writing in October 2022 – that is, in just over two and a half years (Figure 2.1). It is obvious that no individual can read and process all of this information at the rate at which it is produced – that would equate to roughly 335 articles per day just for this topic, each of which might take one to several hours to read. It may even take one to several hours just to skim through an article sufficiently even to know whether it is actually relevant to one's work, let alone to understand completely everything that was done, evaluate it and integrate it with a body of other findings. Thus, sophisticated computational support is urgently needed to detect relevant literature as well as to process the literature automatically and extract relevant information in a way that facilitates the work of researchers and speeds up the process of further scientific discovery.

This chapter surveys the contributions of artificial intelligence technologies to the problems that arise from the management of scientific literature. This includes automated approaches to finding relevant publications, discovering which entities are mentioned in publications and in which combinations, as well as advances towards the more challenging tasks of extracting rich context-specific information from publications, such as determining what the main findings are in each study and how those findings compare to other research, and indeed combining information from several publications. Lastly, the chapter discusses whether artificially intelligent systems for processing scientific literature could go beyond re-discovery to make genuinely novel scientific discoveries in their own right, and explore the future possibilities accompanying alternative platforms to journal articles for scientific dissemination, such as open science knowledge graphs. But first, a closer look at the raw material – the scientific publication itself.

ANATOMY OF A SCIENTIFIC PUBLICATION

While there are differences in practice between different disciplines, the basic outline of a research publication is similar in all domains. Most publications – often called 'papers', even though due to the digital revolution's effects on publishing, most such papers are never printed – have an abstract or summary that presents the background, methods and main findings of the research that is being reported. The remainder of the article presents the same information but at a much greater level of detail. In the introductory part of the publication, the research question that is being asked is usually placed in the context of previous work, and the wider significance of this problem is explained in a way that aims to be accessible to a broad audience. Then, the precise methods are described, including what data were used, how data were collected and how data were interpreted. After that, the results are presented, which may take the form of a table showing the outputs of statistical analyses, as well as visualisations (plots, graphs, illustrations) that summarise, showcase and explain the findings. Finally, the implications of the results are again put in the context of the wider research in the field in a discussion section which may include a comparison to similar work being done by others, and limitations and shortcomings of the particular individual study will ideally be highlighted with a view to informing future studies. In addition, there may be various associated 'supplementary files', which increasingly are also used as a way to share the underlying data associated with the study so that it can be re-used in other research studies – as a part of a move towards greater transparency and reusability of scientific research outputs known as 'open science' (Vicente-Saez and Martinez-Fuentes, 2018).

The branch of artificial intelligence that deals with the automation of the processing of textual content such as the text contained in scientific publications is known as *natural language processing* – because all such texts are written in natural, that is, human, languages. Comprehending natural language has been one of the objectives of artificial intelligence research since the very early days. The first artificial intelligence 'chatbot', ELIZA (Weizenbaum, 1966), could carry out conversations – in a rather narrow and limited scope of pretending to perform 'reflective listening' – that, apparently, could occasionally appear realistic enough for users to think they were communicating with a human being, even though the system only offered a few canned responses or repeated back the input it was given with only a few grammatical changes implemented by rules. However, such a system being able to convince people that a conversation agent involves a human depends in large part on the conversational context and the background and expectations of the people interacting with the system. ELIZA had a very constrained context (what types of conversations it allowed) and, as it was developed in the 1960s, was tested with people who had no background knowledge about how computer systems such as these might be developed.

ELIZA was a forerunner of what is now a significant application area for artificial intelligence technologies: the development of 'chatbots', or automated conversation-based systems that provide support and help, as well as providing specific advice or guidance, in many different contexts on a day-to-day basis. Chatbots have even been developed to provide helpful 'listening' and 'companionship' with objectives such as to reduce loneliness and isolation in vulnerable populations, and it is intriguing to explore the ways in which humans establish and experience relationships with such artificial agents (Skjuve et al., 2021), even while knowing that they are artificial. Even within the context of an 'as if' or explicitly pretend quality to a human-machine relationship, it appears that at least some of the social-cognitive aspects of human relational psychology are engaged (Ta-Johnson *et al.*, 2022). We might hypothesise that the more sophisticated such conversational agents become, the more this is likely to be the case.

Quite recently, a debate in the popular media about whether or not artificial intelligence-driven chatbot systems were, or could appear to be, 'sentient', was sparked by a Google engineer admitting in an interview that he had a sense, during his interactions with one of Google's large advanced conversational models, that the model had become sentient (Luscombe, 2022). The engineer, who was subsequently suspended, described the system as showing evidence of thoughts and feelings of an equivalent level to those that a human child might have. For example, the system reported having a fear of death, when prompted to think how it might feel if it would be switched off. However, such systems are trained on human texts as their inputs, and they learn to respond to prompts based on how humans have answered questions. Thus, it is not surprising that they report fear of death just as a human might. That should, however, not be taken as evidence of self-awareness – paradoxically, true self-awareness in an artificial system would surely lead to *less* human-like thoughts and feelings.

But this question is a digression: what can be confidently asserted is that since the early days of natural language processing, the methods involved in processing natural language have advanced significantly. And for scientific literature management, they are absolutely needed.

LITERATURE DISCOVERY AND TERM EXTRACTION

The first challenge that researchers might face when embarking on a scientific study is to identify everything that is already known, which will in practice mean that the researchers will need to survey the published scientific literature relevant to their research question and methodology. Just to find all the relevant publications on a topic is already an immense challenge, given the volumes of scientific literature already published, and being published every day, and this is exacerbated by the fact that no single repository or search engine encompasses all of the relevant literature, in particular when considering all contributions in all languages distributed around the world.

SIMPLE INDEXING

The first part of this challenge is to index and associate each newly published resource with metadata that supports primary discoverability (retrieving the right results when searching). For example, all research pertaining to COVID-19 should be returned when a user types 'COVID-19' into a literature search index. Insofar as this task entails basic matching of strings (terms or small phrases), it doesn't require intelligence, just complete data access and processing power adequate to handling the volumes involved. The most straightforward of this type of system work just on titles and abstracts, indexing the words and phrases that appear therein. However, there are almost always multiple ways to describe or refer to any entity that is the subject of a scientific investigation, so associating rich metadata such as synonyms and controlled vocabularies of standard entity labels is essential for search results to be more complete. There are several indexing services and databases that amass literature references. For example, the PubMed resource collects biomedical domain literature (PubMed, no date), while the open literature index aggregator OpenAlex (OpenAlex: The open catalog to the global research system, 2022) provides open access to a wide range of scientific publications indexed by keywords and, where available, the most common words in the abstract. However, there is some evidence that existing indexing services are not always keeping up with the pace of publication (Larsen and von Ins, 2010), and even if keeping up to date, they are in many cases not sufficiently well annotated with organising metadata to support comprehensive search and discovery (Gough, Thomas and Oliver, 2019). This is a problem of scale and complexity beyond what humans can handle, thus, it is a fantastic opportunity for artificially intelligent systems that are able to track and automatically index emerging publications and support intelligent search mechanisms in order to enhance discovery.

DISAMBIGUATING REFERENCES

However, detecting the right literature pertaining to a given research study usually involves more than just matching strings or finding keywords. This is because most words and even combinations of words are not exact enough to find very specific research reports, and on the other hand, if research is described with very specific and uncommon terminology then it may be that this uncommon expression is not indexed.

Consider how a typical Google search works for individuals. Finding a specific person who has a very common name is usually difficult, without knowing additional information that helps disambiguate the individual, such as where they are located. However, finding a very famous person, for whom a vast number of search results are available, is usually easy even if they have a common name, but then the volumes of results that will be returned will prohibit an exhaustive processing. (Although, unlike in scientific literature searches, exhaustive processing is not usually the objective of a Google search.) And finding a person who has a very rare name but who is sufficiently present on webpages that are popular enough to at least have been indexed is also easy. But the vast majority of people are neither famous enough to be the top-ranked hits for their names nor have names that are rare enough to be distinctive but nevertheless prominent enough to have been indexed. Thus, most people are not easy to find with a Google search for their names.

It is similar for most terminology related to scientific research. To take an example, let's consider a researcher working to discover a new therapeutic direction for the condition schizophrenia. The body of literature that broadly pertains to this question is huge: searching for 'schizophrenia' and 'therapy' on PubMed generates

68,300 results. Given that the new therapeutic approach is not yet known in the literature, the objective of the search might be to find similar approaches that have been tried before. But the variety of ways that such approaches might have been described is not constrained to a set of keywords. Narrowing the long list of reports down to those that are specifically relevant for a given research study thus does require intelligence. And systems based on artificial intelligence technologies are slowly rising to this task – artificial intelligence-based literature search tools are becoming more common, although many are commercial (Extance, 2018).

We might break down the overall problem into several different challenges. The first such challenge for an automated literature processing system is to correctly disambiguate and find examples of references to entities of a particular type in the literature, in order to be able to sort and index papers based on what type of entity they are about, and to retrieve examples of passages referring to entities of those types. In an expression popularised by Google when it introduced a facility for entity type disambiguation for its search results, we might say that we are going beyond 'strings' to 'things' (Singhal, 2012). The introduction of a facility for entity type disambiguation in its search results allowed Google to distinguish between, for example, 'Taj Mahal' as the building, and a human being who happened to be named 'Taj Mahal'. For a more scientific example, a word such as 'cell' has many different meanings in different scientific contexts – it may represent a unit of an energy storage battery, or a part of a living organism, or a mobile phone. Humans use *context* to decide between plausible references for labels such as 'cell' in the context of given passages of text and disambiguate what the things are that are intended to be referred to, typically without even noticing the alternative out-of-context interpretation of a given word or phrase. But for artificial systems to be able to correctly disambiguate references to different sorts of thing is not a trivial task at all.

Natural language processing methods for entity semantic type and reference disambiguation have been developed in particular for the biomedical sciences, where the nature of the subject material means that it is advantageous to be able to track literature by entity type. For example, there are artificial intelligence-based systems to recognize mentions of chemicals (e.g., Hemati and Mehler, 2019), proteins (Zhou *et al.*, 2020) and diseases (Wang and Akella, 2015) in text. Systems that determine multiple semantic types at the same time may need to distinguish, for example, between the chemical entity 'alcohol' and the protein (enzyme) 'alcohol dehydrogenase'. Such systems are already operating in practice, such as within the literature indexing service Europe PubMedCentral (Ferguson *et al.*, 2021), helping to organise and catalogue the scientific literature and allow more advanced searching and indexing. However, similar services are less common in domains outside of biomedicine, such as the social and behavioural sciences, where the use of shared computable vocabularies is as yet somewhat less common (Hastings *et al.*, 2021).

EVALUATION OF ARTIFICIAL INTELLIGENCE SYSTEMS

For the development of artificial intelligence systems, it is important that they be able to be evaluated in a consistent way, so that different systems aiming to address the same challenge can be compared, and also so that the performance of such systems can be reported in ways that can be transparently assessed so that consumers are not misled about the capabilities of the system. The way that this is typically done is by comparing the predictions of the automated system to a previously prepared 'gold standard' that has been created by humans. So, for example, if the task is to decide whether mentions of the string label 'cell' refer to a battery component or biological entity, the system might be evaluated using examples of sentences containing such strings which have been annotated with the relevant entity sense by humans. The prediction of the sense generated by the machine will then be compared to the 'gold standard' sense annotated by the humans. This comparison allows for the generation of standard metrics of success, such as the percentage of accurate predictions. However, it is worth noting as an aside, that some problems can be challenging even for humans to reliably agree on what is the correct annotation to make in a given context, thus, the performance of the artificial system should also be compared to the baseline agreement level between human experts who are asked to perform the same task.

RELATIONSHIP EXTRACTION AND KNOWLEDGE GRAPHS

Assuming that entity references in text are being recognised and disambiguated correctly, the next challenge for natural language processing of scientific texts is to be able to recognise specific relationships between entity mentions that are specified in the text. Considering the previously described example of searching for therapeutic approaches that target schizophrenia as a condition, there are two entities involved – one a therapeutic approach, the other a condition – and a relationship between them, which we might call targeting or treating. Detecting the nature of the relationship that a given scientific paper is reporting between entities is often crucially important for correctly evaluating what the article is about, and can be very tricky for artificial systems to achieve since it can depend on complex nested meaning structures.

Often, for downstream analyses, the wordy and bulky scientific publication is not the most convenient format. It would be easier to have the entities and their relationships (facts) directly accessible in a computable format for processing and use in searching and indexing, data-driven investigations, statistical processing and as a knowledge base for answering questions. For these purposes, data from verbose natural language may be extracted in the form of succinct entity-relationship-entity 'triples' which are taken together to form a *knowledge graph* populated from the processed literature. One example of such a literature-populated knowledge graph in biomedicine is called SPOKE (Nelson, Butte and Baranzini, 2019) or the 'Scalable precision medicine open knowledge engine', which integrates a hugely complex set of references to entities of different types.

The resulting knowledge graph can be queried and interactively explored, and even supports the prediction of potential inferred 'missing links', which can be used, for example, to suggest drugs that can be repurposed to treat additional diseases (Himmelstein *et al.*, 2017). Any kind of entity can be the subject of a knowledge graph – even the literature itself, as evidenced by an example of a knowledge graph about COVID-19 literature that contains representations of scientific publications alongside the facts that can be extracted from them (Pestryakova *et al.*, 2022).

OTHER TASKS IN THE MANAGEMENT OF SCIENTIFIC LITERATURE

Going beyond identifying specific entities and relationships, there are a wealth of additional tasks in the management of the scientific literature for which artificial intelligence can provide support. For example, we may wish to identify relevant sections in papers in the scientific literature that are most relevant for answering a specific question – which we might recognise as another task that Google's search engine performs, at least for some search results. Ought, an organisation that develops artificial intelligence technologies, recently released a tool called Elicit, described as an artificial intelligence 'research assistant' – a literature query engine that is able to parse queries in natural language and find articles that appear to provide an answer to that query.

Another additional task is that we may wish to find papers that are similar to a given paper or set of papers that we are interested in. The system 'Iris.ai' (*Iris.ai - Your Researcher Workspace – Leading AI for your research challenge,* 2022) creates a map of related papers using document fingerprints which are made up of a transformation of the words in the document into a sequence of numbers, which then allows the definition of a quantitative measure of similarity for papers. Similarity measures for publications can also be used to summarise or cluster whole subsections within the overall body of literature on a topic, in what is known as 'topic modelling'. For example, in Scaccia and Scott

(2021), abstracts from the journal Implementation Science were clustered and explored using an artificial intelligence-based approach to identify the top topics in the journal over the entire history of the journal as well as how the topic areas had changed over time.

For an even more complex task, we may wish to identify what the specific findings are that a given study provides evidence in support of, and what that evidential support is, as distinct from sentences in the paper that refer to background knowledge and findings cited from previous work. This involves being able to separate out the background and contextual information that is presented in a publication from what is specifically novel and presented in the main results section of any given publication, and then being able to identify how the novel findings are supported by the evidence. This very challenging task brings us to the processing of the scientific literature not only as a collection of texts in which sentences report arbitrary claims but also as studies in which evidence for specific claims is examined and then findings are reported. In other words, we come to approaches that engage with the literature not just as text but actively engage with what the scientific literature actually is – that is, as reports of *evidence*.

EVIDENCE AND ITS SYNTHESIS

Scientific discoveries are composed of a series of inferences from data to conclusions that are described in scientific publications. Typically, scientific publications have a logical structure that aims to make a logical case for concluding the claims that the paper is supporting on the basis of the evidence presented. Of course, the structure of such arguments and the nature of the supporting evidence are discipline-specific. However, there are overarching patterns in argumentation structure that reflect ordinary human logical reasoning capabilities, and which a sophisticated artificial intelligence system should be able to detect.

Systems that are artificially able to detect and process argumentation structure in scientific publications do not yet exist, although early frontrunners of such systems with limited capabilities are being developed (e.g., Lauscher *et al.*, 2018). In general, current approaches to artificial intelligence which rely on machine learning to perform natural language processing tasks are limited in their capability to learn logical reasoning (Santoro *et al.*, 2021) – while approaches to artificial intelligence which are based on directly implemented symbolic systems and inference engines struggle to map elegantly onto the vagueness and flexibility of human natural languages. It is fascinating that humans are able to switch between and integrate across these capabilities without (for the most part) even noticing that we are doing so.

In the health sciences, scientific discovery has direct practical implications, and we often have an interest in the outcomes of research that goes beyond curiosity into guiding actions. For example, a large fraction of health-related research evaluates *interventions* for how well they work, and reports *outcomes* that may inform policies and practice. For example, one might study whether increasing physical activity is effective in improving mental health (O'Donoghue, 2021), or whether one drug is more effective than another in treating a disease such as COVID-19. In order to answer questions such as these, it is of course necessary to find all the relevant publications that provide evidence that can help to answer the question, but even then, once most or all of the relevant publications have been determined, it is still unlikely that they all report identical results. Rather, each study that is conducted, even when trying to answer the same question, uses a slightly different approach and may have a different population, intervention, context, outcome or other study variables. It may thus be tricky to arrive at a comprehensive *synthesised* overview of a whole body of research on a given topic, even if all the relevant publications have been discovered.

The process of extracting and combining reported data across studies to create a holistic and integrated body of evidence to answer a particular question or set of questions is known as *evidence synthesis* (Cochrane, 2022). The process of searching for evidence to support one or another answer to a given question is called conducting a *systematic review.* The statistical methodologies by which data from different studies are combined in order to answer overarching questions across the full range of available studies are called *meta-analyses.* Systematic reviews have become the gold standard for evidence across many different domains (Cochrane, 2022) and are conducted for many different purposes (Gough, Thomas and Oliver, 2019). There are different types of reviews for different questions and types of evidence. The Cochrane Database of Systematic Reviews, a prominent collection of systematic reviews, specifies the following types (*About Cochrane Reviews | Cochrane Library,* no date):

- *Intervention reviews* assess the effectiveness or safety of a treatment, vaccine, device, preventative measure, procedure or policy.
- *Diagnostic test accuracy reviews* assess the accuracy of a test, device or scale to aid diagnosis.
- *Prognosis reviews* describe and predict the course of individuals with a disease or health condition.
- *Qualitative evidence syntheses* investigate perspectives and experiences of an intervention or health condition.
- *Methodology reviews* explore or validate how research is designed, conducted, reported or used.
- *Overviews of reviews* synthesise information from multiple systematic reviews on related research questions.
- *Rapid reviews* are systematic reviews accelerated through streamlining or omitting specific methods.
- *Prototype reviews* include other types of systematic review that do not yet have established standard methodology in Cochrane, such as scoping reviews, mixed-methods reviews, reviews of prevalence studies and realist reviews.

Conducting systematic reviews and meta-analyses is a slow and laborious manual process, often taking months or years from start to end, creating an urgent need for the improved automation that artificial intelligence-based systems can offer. Moreover, systematic reviews also start to become outdated when they are published, thus, there is a great need for living systematic reviews (Elliott *et al.*, 2021) – systematic reviews that are kept up to date – and again, there is a foreseen role of automation and artificial intelligence technologies in achieving this (Thomas *et al.*, 2017).

But can an artificial intelligence-based system be developed that comprehensively integrates across a whole body of evidence and keeps itself up to date? The Human Behaviour-Change Project (Michie *et al.*, 2020a) is an ambitious project in the domain of evidence about human behaviour that aims to create an artificial intelligence-based system able to automatically scan the global world's published reports of behavioural intervention evaluations, extract and analyse relevant information in those reports, and use the extracted information to answer specific queries about what works to change behaviour, indicating the level of confidence in the answers and explaining the process. The project consists of a complex set of interrelated automation components including a module to identify new publications of the right type (randomised controlled trials), modules to extract structured data from reports describing the attributes of interventions and comparator groups and the outcomes, and a prediction module based on machine learning that synthesizes the evidence from the reports and learns to predict outcomes for interventions. The automation components are supported by the development of a comprehensive ontology (Hastings, 2017) or formal representational structure for the domain of behaviour change interventions (Michie *et al.*, 2020b), which describes the structure of a behaviour change intervention and its many different components, and supplies the vocabulary and semantics that in turn are used by the automated functions.

Work on this project is still ongoing at the time of writing, and early evaluation findings show clear evidence that some parts of the problem are less amenable to automation with currently available technologies than others. This should not surprise us: it is to be expected that in such an ambitious project, some parts of the overall task will be empirically determined to be out of reach for our current generation of artificial intelligence technologies. But there is no question that systems such as this are urgently needed, and the findings are thus valuable both in terms of the project's successes and also in terms of clarifying the limitations of the current generation of technology so as to pave the way for the developments of the future.

By integrating multiple individual components made up of the sorts of artificial intelligence systems surveyed in this chapter, artificial technologies are moving closer to being able to operate as 'robot scientific assistant literature managers' – surveying the published literature and amassing an overview of what the literature says about a given topic. However, their applicability thus far is limited to quite narrow domains, specific types of questions and specific types of assistance, heavily skewed towards biomedicine, for which the human systems supporting literature management such as annotations to controlled vocabularies are also in more widespread use.

BEYOND RE-DISCOVERY: MAKING DISCOVERIES BASED ON LITERATURE

Supporting finding, indexing, aggregating and answering questions based on the scientific literature, however difficult these challenges are (and they are difficult), still only count as a very partial assistance for the scientific processes involved in the scientific literature. Going beyond *re-discovery* is an essential frontier for the use of artificial intelligence in science (Krenn *et al.*, 2022).

The scientific literature is the primary documentary record of scientific discoveries. But it can itself also be a source for new scientific discoveries – it can itself become the data source about which questions are asked and answered. One such question that researchers have asked of the scientific literature is, can an artificial intelligence-based system trained on scientific article texts predict future discoveries? Is the next discovery hiding in plain sight in the publications that are already published, if we just know how to look?

In one recent study, an artificial intelligence system was trained to recognise mentions of chemicals and their properties in materials science (Tshitoyan *et al.*, 2019). The authors then compared the predictions of the system trained on past publications to demonstrate that the system was able to predict materials suitable for specific functional applications years before those materials were, in fact, linked with those functional applications (as represented in later publications).

In another study, an artificial intelligence system was trained to predict which genes would receive interest for a particular therapeutic domain next (Serrano Nájera, Narganes Carlón and Crowther, 2021). This pipeline uses the networks of papers citing each other, and papers being cited together, alongside mentions of genes and disease types. Then a neural network is trained to predict the dynamics associated with publications mentioning the human genes, with genes of higher interest being identified per therapeutic focus area. The methods of topic detection are used to provide suggested 'reasons' why a particular gene is achieving higher interest in a particular therapeutic domain area. The system also proposes the most important review articles for a potential target, based on the citation information. Using historical snapshots of publications at earlier points in historical time, the ability of this system to predict the future was probed, and then a metric of 'trendiness' was assigned to some genes, defined as when the actual publications exceeded the expected (predicted) publications in a way for which the model cannot account. The topics extracted from the topic detection algorithm projected onto timelines were then used to help to explain the emergence of these trends.

However, only time will tell whether this system can provide actionable recommendations about the future that is yet to come. Thus far, we tend to evaluate algorithms by showing that they can re-discover laws or findings that we already know to hold – with the result that thus far, such hypotheses as have been generated by artificial intelligence systems have mostly been of the unsurprising sort. Even if such systems can be shown to re-predict discoveries in recent history, that is not the same as being shown to be able to predict discoveries that then truly occur in the future. The famous Niels

Bohr quote comes to mind – 'prediction is very difficult, especially if it's about the future!'

REFERENCES

About Cochrane Reviews | Cochrane Library (no date). Available at: https://www. cochranelibrary.com/about/about-cochrane-reviews (Accessed: 21 October 2022).

Bornmann, L., Haunschild, R. and Mutz, R. (2021) 'Growth rates of modern science: A latent piecewise growth curve approach to model publication numbers from established and new literature databases', *Humanities and Social Sciences Communications*, 8(1), pp. 1–15. Available at: https://doi.org/10.1057/s41599-021-00903-w.

Bornmann, L. and Mutz, R. (2015) 'Growth rates of modern science: A bibliometric analysis based on the number of publications and cited references', *Journal of the Association for Information Science and Technology*, 66(11), pp. 2215–2222. Available at: https://doi.org/10.1002/asi.23329.

Cochrane (2022) *Evidence synthesis - What is it and why do we need it?* Available at: https://www.cochrane.org/news/evidence-synthesis-what-it-and-why-do-we-need-it (Accessed: 13 April 2022).

Elliott, J. *et al.* (2021) 'Decision makers need constantly updated evidence synthesis', *Nature*, 600(7889), pp. 383–385. Available at: https://doi.org/10.1038/d41586-021-03690-1.

Extance, A. (2018) 'How AI technology can tame the scientific literature', *Nature*, 561(7722), pp. 273–274. Available at: https://doi.org/10.1038/d41586-018-06617-5.

Ferguson, C. *et al.* (2021) 'Europe PMC in 2020', *Nucleic Acids Research*, 49(D1), pp. D1507–D1514. Available at: https://doi.org/10.1093/nar/gkaa994.

Gough, D., Thomas, J. and Oliver, S. (2019) 'Clarifying differences between reviews within evidence ecosystems', *Systematic Reviews*, 8(1), p. 170. Available at: https://doi.org/10.1186/s13643-019-1089-2.

Hastings, J. (2017) 'Primer on Ontologies', in C. Dessimoz and N. Škunca (eds) *The Gene Ontology Handbook*. New York, NY: Springer New York (Methods in Molecular Biology), pp. 3–13. Available at: https://doi.org/10.1007/978-1-4939-3743-1_1.

Hastings, J. *et al.* (2021) 'Ontologies for the Behavioural and Social Sciences: Opportunities and Challenges', in J. Hastings and A. Barton (eds) *Proceedings* of the International Conference on Biomedical Ontologies 2021. International Conference on Biomedical Ontologies 2021, Bozen-Bolzano, Italy: CEUR (CEUR Workshop Proceedings), pp. 155–161. Available at: http://ceur-ws.org/Vol-3073/#invited1 (Accessed: 6 February 2022).

Hemati, W. and Mehler, A. (2019) 'LSTMVoter: Chemical named entity recognition using a conglomerate of sequence labeling tools', Journal of Cheminformatics, 11(1), p. 3. Available at: https://doi.org/10.1186/s13321-018-0327-2.

Himmelstein, D.S. et al. (2017) 'Systematic integration of biomedical knowledge prioritizes drugs for repurposing', eLife. Edited by A. Valencia, 6, p. e26726. Available at: https://doi.org/10.7554/eLife.26726.

Iris.ai - Your Researcher Workspace – Leading AI for your research challenge (2022) Iris.ai - Your Researcher Workspace. Available at: https://iris.ai/ (Accessed: 12 July 2022).

Krenn, M. et al. (2022) 'On scientific understanding with artificial intelligence', arXiv:2204.01467 [physics] [Preprint]. Available at: http://arxiv.org/abs/2204.01467 (Accessed: 5 April 2022).

Larsen, P.O. and von Ins, M. (2010) 'The rate of growth in scientific publication and the decline in coverage provided by Science Citation Index', Scientometrics, 84(3), pp. 575–603. Available at: https://doi.org/10.1007/s11192-010-0202-z.

Lauscher, A. et al. (2018) 'Investigating the Role of Argumentation in the Rhetorical Analysis of Scientific Publications With Neural Multi-Task Learning Models', in E. Riloff (ed). 2018 Conference on Empirical Methods in Natural Language Processing, Stroudsburg, PA: Association for Computational Linguistics, pp. 3326–3338. Available at: https://madoc.bib.uni-mannheim.de/46086 (Accessed: 12 July 2022).

Luscombe, R. (2022) Google engineer put on leave after saying AI chatbot has become sentient | Google | The Guardian. Available at: https://www.theguardian.com/technology/2022/jun/12/google-engineer-ai-bot-sentient-blake-lemoine (Accessed: 11 July 2022).

Michie, S., et al. (2020a) 'The human behaviour-change project: An artificial intelligence system to answer questions about changing behaviour', Wellcome Open Research, 5, p. 122. Available at: https://doi.org/10.12688/wellcomeopenres.15900.1.

Michie, S. et al. (2020b) 'Representation of behaviour change interventions and their evaluation: Development of the upper level of the behaviour change intervention ontology', Wellcome Open Research, 5, p. 123. Available at: https://doi.org/10.12688/wellcomeopenres.15902.1.

Nelson, C.A., Butte, A.J. and Baranzini, S.E. (2019) 'Integrating biomedical research and electronic health records to create knowledge-based biologically meaningful machine-readable embeddings', *Nature Communications*, 10(1), p. 3045. Available at: https://doi.org/10.1038/s41467-019-11069-0.

O'Donoghue, B. (2021) 'Addressing physical health in mental illness: The urgent need to translate evidence-based interventions into routine clinical practice', *Irish Journal of Psychological Medicine*, 38(1), pp. 1–5. Available at: https://doi.org/10.1017/ipm.2021.4.

OpenAlex: The open catalog to the global research system (2022) Available at: https://open alex.org/ (Accessed: 11 July 2022).

Pestryakova, S. *et al.* (2022) 'COVIDPUBGRAPH: A FAIR knowledge graph of COVID-19 publications', *Scientific Data*, 9(1), p. 389. Available at: https://doi.org/10.1038/s41597-022-01298-2.

PubMed (no date) *PubMed*. Available at: https://pubmed.ncbi.nlm.nih.gov/ (Accessed: 11 July 2022).

Santoro, A. *et al.* (2021) 'Symbolic Behaviour in Artificial Intelligence', *arXiv:2102.03406 [cs]* [Preprint]. Available at: http://arxiv.org/abs/2102.03406 (Accessed: 6 May 2021).

Scaccia, J.P. and Scott, V.C. (2021) '5335 days of implementation science: Using natural language processing to examine publication trends and topics', *Implementation Science*, 16(1), p. 47. Available at: https://doi.org/10.1186/s13012-021-01120-4.

Serrano Nájera, G., Narganes Carlón, D. and Crowther, D.J. (2021) 'TrendyGenes, a computational pipeline for the detection of literature trends in academia and drug discovery', *Scientific Reports*, 11(1), p. 15747. Available at: https://doi.org/10.1038/s41598-021-94897-9.

Singhal, A. (2012) *Introducing the knowledge graph: Things, not strings, Google*. Available at: https://blog.google/products/search/introducing-knowledge-graph-things-not/ (Accessed: 25 February 2021).

Skjuve, M. *et al.* (2021) 'My chatbot companion - a study of human-chatbot relationships', *International Journal of Human-Computer Studies*, 149, p. 102601. Available at: https://doi.org/10.1016/j.ijhcs.2021.102601.

Ta-Johnson, V.P. *et al.* (2022) 'Assessing the topics and motivating factors behind human-social chatbot interactions: Thematic analysis of user experiences', *JMIR Human Factors*, 9(4), p. e38876. Available at: https://doi.org/10.2196/38876.

Thomas, J. *et al.* (2017) 'Living systematic reviews: 2. Combining human and machine effort', *Journal of Clinical Epidemiology*, 91, pp. 31–37. Available at: https://doi.org/10.1016/j.jclinepi.2017.08.011.

Tshitoyan, V. *et al.* (2019) 'Unsupervised word embeddings capture latent knowledge from materials science literature', *Nature*, 571(7763), pp. 95–98. Available at: https://doi.org/10.1038/s41586-019-1335-8.

van Raan, A.F.J. (2004) 'Measuring Science: Capita Selecta of Current Main Issues', in H.F. Moed, W. Glänzel and U. Schmoch (eds) *Handbook of Quantitative Science and Technology Research*. Dordrecht: Springer Netherlands, pp. 19–50. Available at: https://doi.org/10.1007/1-4020-2755-9_2.

Vicente-Saez, R. and Martinez-Fuentes, C. (2018) 'Open science now: A systematic literature review for an integrated definition', *Journal of Business Research*, 88, pp. 428–436. Available at: https://doi.org/10.1016/j.jbusres.2017.12.043.

Wang, C. and Akella, R. (2015) 'A hybrid approach to extracting disorder mentions from clinical notes', *AMIA Summits on Translational Science Proceedings*, 2015, pp. 183–187.

Weizenbaum, J. (1966) 'ELIZA— a computer program for the study of natural language communication between man and machine', *Communications of the ACM*, 9(1), pp. 36–45. Available at: https://doi.org/10.1145/365153.365168.

Zhou, H. *et al.* (2020) 'Knowledge-enhanced biomedical named entity recognition and normalization: Application to proteins and genes', *BMC Bioinformatics*, 21(1), p. 35. Available at: https://doi.org/10.1186/s12859-020-3375-3.

3

AI FOR DATA INTERPRETATION

At the turn of the 21st century, biology underwent a step change in its existence as a disciplinary field of research, with the publication of the first full draft of the human genome (Lander *et al.*, 2001). This project, which involved computational support from its inception, heralded the arrival of an age of 'big data' in biology – and the pace of data generation has only accelerated since then. By now there are a whole family of different types of large-scale measurements that are routinely used in biological research to measure different aspects of the genome and its downstream products such as transcripts and proteins in living cells. And, while the first human genome took a decade to complete, similarly large-scale measurements of sequences today can be completed within a few hours. Such measurements may map out the sequence itself: a typical human genome consists of around 3 billion 'base pairs', that is, complementary nucleotide bases that pair together to build the double helix of the genome. Alternatively, the measurements may be of the abundances of down-stream biomolecules, whose synthesis in the cell may be directly or indirectly controlled by the genome. Unlike the genome, the abundances of biomolecules can change from time to time and condition to condition, necessitating multiple measurements to understand the overall variability and to enable statistical comparisons within and between biological samples. These biomolecules may be proteins: there are around 20,000–25,000 protein-coding genes within the

DOI: 10.1201/9781003226642-3

human genome, each of which may have multiple alternative forms. Alternatively, the biomolecules may be metabolites, the small molecules present in biological systems that participate in all metabolic and systemic processes: there may be tens of thousands of different metabolites present in any given biological sample. And there are thousands of such samples being measured every day at institutes around the world, at a pace of data generation that is only accelerating over time (Marx, 2013).

Biology is not alone in facing the challenge of exponentially growing volumes of data to interpret: almost all scientific disciplines are facing a similar situation, including physics (which faced big data challenges even before biology did), the environmental sciences, psychology and the broader social sciences. Astronomy (Zhang and Zhao, 2015), to name one example, is intrinsically a big data discipline, with a wide range of telescopes distributed across the planet and in the nearby planetary neighbourhood, each of which generates petabytes of information, which is then stored and exchanged for researchers to harness globally. Modern climate science (Sebestyén, Czvetkó and Abonyi, 2021), for another pertinent example, generates huge volumes of data during the process of tracking, monitoring and making predictions about our globally changing climate in response to changing human activities and emissions. The emerging science of continuous monitoring for health promotion in humans (Hicks *et al.*, 2019), collecting measurements via everyday devices and mobile phone applications, is yet another example area where enormous datasets are being generated, stored and exchanged on a daily basis. In each of these example domains, and many, many more besides, the volumes of data being generated, stored and interpreted exceed what would have been imaginable only a few decades ago. Given the volumes, computational support is absolutely essential for their storage, management, interpretation and manipulation. But going beyond 'mere' computational support, we might wonder what frontiers are opened by the application of artificial intelligence algorithms to the challenge of making sense of these data?

A vision for a truly intelligent artificial agent supporting data-driven discovery might be that such an agent would be able to simultaneously process multiple data streams of diverse types arising from different sources, effortlessly spot patterns and meanings in the data, highlighting actionable trends and discoveries that are the most relevant and significant, integrating the new data into the background context of the theoretical knowledge of the domain, and returning with actionable suggestions for appropriate inferences. Of course, such a powerful artificial system does not yet exist (and perhaps can never exist). Nevertheless, alongside the advances in volumes and varieties of data, are essential advances in the algorithms used to process the data, without which many of the recent discoveries in these fields would not have been possible.

MAKING PREDICTIONS FROM DATA

One of the primary purposes of artificial intelligence algorithms that learn from data is to make predictions. These predictions might be straightforwardly about the future, as in the case of the science of climate change: given all the world's historical measurements of temperatures, atmospheric gas concentrations, weather patterns and so on, can we predict what the climate of the future will be like? Or, for another example: throughout the unfolding of the COVID-19 pandemic, practical predictions became utterly essential for the smooth running of healthcare facilities in unprecedented times. For example, there was a need to predict how many hospital beds for COVID patients would be required in one week, or two weeks' time, given the current evolution of the virus and the governmental measures implemented (Turbé *et al.*, 2021). Could we predict how much oxygen would be required? How soon will the next wave of infections strike? The pandemic provided (and still provides) a wealth of opportunities to test algorithmic data-driven predictions in practice. It also showcased the limitations of such approaches – prediction of the future always depends not only on extrapolating from the data that is available about the past but also on assumptions and knowledge about what might be different in the future.

There are some aspects of the world that are inherently very predictable, given the knowledge we have today together with our capabilities to measure and acquire data. For example, we can predict with great confidence the positions of the planets in the night sky as they shift in their orbits around the sun, or when the next solar eclipse is due to be visible and from where. We can predict with reasonable confidence the time it will take to drive or walk along a predefined route (assuming average traffic conditions), and how many people will buy a house next month (assuming average market conditions).

But there are other problems for which even with huge amounts of available data, and even though the problem *seems* as though it ought to be predictable because similar inputs lead reliably to similar outputs, the predictive performance of even our best algorithms has historically been poor. One such problem, until 2021, was protein folding.

PREDICTING HOW PROTEINS WILL FOLD

Proteins are the basic building blocks of living organisms. They are built from instructions encoded in the genome by specialised translational machinery in almost every cell of the body. Each protein consists of sequences of amino acids, chemically bonded together into lengthy chains, which then fold up into a myriad of unique three-dimensional shapes. In general, with very high repeatability, the same type of protein, containing the same amino acid sequence, will form exactly the same three-dimensional shape. The process by which the amino acid sequence forms its final shape is called protein folding. For many years, scientists have been searching for a way to predict the eventual shape of a protein from its amino acid sequence (Dill *et al.*, 2008). This is because the shape is needed to predict many other aspects of how the protein will interact with its biological environment, what it will be able to do, and indeed what types of drugs might be designed to work with it (to enhance its activity) or against it (to reduce its activity) to achieve specific outcomes in health or in disease. The sequence of the protein in terms of which amino acids it is made up of can be predicted with high faithfulness directly from the sequence of the genome, which advances in technology have enabled us to measure for an enormous diversity of different organisms. However, the shape that those proteins will form is still difficult to measure with our current technologies, as most technologies for measuring the final shape of a folded protein require crystallisation of the protein structure, a procedure that is experimentally challenging, and not possible for all protein structures. As a result, there are close to 200 million protein sequences in leading protein sequence databases, but only around 190,000 experimentally determined protein structures (RSCB Protein Data Bank, 2022). Thus, being able to predict the shape of the folded protein from the sequence has long been an objective of algorithmic development in biological science.

However, for a long time, the predictive performance of such systems was poor. Even though the same sequence typically leads to the same three-dimensional structure, being able to determine in advance what that structure would be based only on the sequence information did not work very well.

Importantly, the way that such algorithms are evaluated is based on comparing predicted structures (shapes) generated with different prediction systems to a collection of recently experimentally measured but not yet published structures in an annual competition (Kryshtafovych, Monastyrskyy and Fidelis, 2016). The fact that the predictions are made and submitted before the structures are publicly released ensures that there is no accidental leakage of relevant information into the prediction model since the data for the predicted cases is not available until after the competition. The performance of competing models in predicting structures is scored based on how close the predicted structures are to the real structures in a score out of 100. Typically, the performance of predictive algorithms in the competition in recent years did not exceed 50 out of 100. However, in 2021, an artificial intelligence-based system called AlphaFold (Jumper *et al.*, 2021), developed by the company DeepMind which had also previously developed winning game-playing systems, was able to achieve a median score of 87 in the competition, far outperforming the best performance of the next best algorithm. This accuracy level was for the first time sufficient to enable downstream biological research to make use of the predicted structures. And as an additional benefit, the system assigns a confidence score to each part of the overall predicted structure, so that it is possible to tell which parts of the prediction the system was able to predict more reliably, compared to those that it found harder to predict – which may involve intrinsically less tightly constrained regions in which the structure has greater flexibility.

The AlphaFold system is a trained model which has learned to make the predictions that it makes from vast amounts of data. It has been trained on the entire collection of known protein sequences and known folded structures across all organisms, including the information about which parts of the sequences are close together in the final folded structure. The predictions it makes thus depend on the fact that the sequence and folded structure information is available – that the data is accessible in the public domain and reusable for this purpose. But the sequences and structures were not all the data that AlphaFold uses to make its predictions. In addition to the data about sequence-to-structure relationships, the system uses information about how similar sequences are across different types of organisms so that it can harness the information that similar sequences in different organisms usually fold similarly as well (Figure 3.1). Moreover, in addition to the part of the system that is based on machine learning directly from data, the system also uses knowledge-based information about the possible geometry of the types of shapes that such sequence-based structures can physically form, in order to exclude any potential predicted conformations that would, in fact, violate physical geometric constraints.

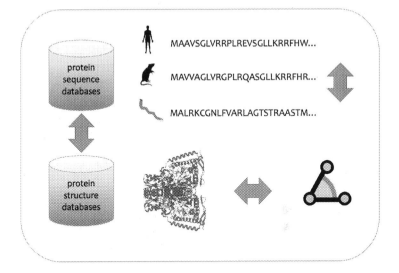

Figure 3.1   Data harnessed by the AlphaFold system: known protein sequence-to-structure relationships across the full range of different protein families and organisms are combined with information about sequence alignments between protein sequences for the same protein in different organisms, and information about conformational possibilities for the three-dimensional folded structure. The illustration shows the first part of the sequence for a part of the *pyruvate dehydrogenase* protein in human, mouse and worm and an illustration of the three-dimensional structure of the same protein in humans.

The resulting highly complex model was able to predict protein structures for nearly a million human proteins, which have now been made freely available in an open online database (*AlphaFold Protein Structure Database*, 2022), in a similarly open fashion as the underlying sequence and structure data on which the predictive model is based. Thus, AlphaFold provides a salient example of the best way in which artificial intelligence technology can be used to accelerate scientific discovery – by addressing a specific bottle-neck in an overall scientific process, learning from existing data to make predictions that lead to new knowledge and insights, and contributing those back to the scientific community in order to drive further discoveries down the line.

The AlphaFold example is one in which the output of the artificial intelligence algorithm was a prediction, a transformation, in essence generating more data of a different form from the data that were already available. But algorithms can also be used to accelerate scientific discovery in ways that more closely relate to the core process of scientific discovery – the *interpretation* of data.

DISCOVERING PATTERNS AND MEANINGS IN DATA

Data analysis is the process of searching for patterns and meanings in data, of going from data to interpretation, of deciding, based on the data available, what that data are suggesting might be the answer to a scientific question. Galileo famously asked whether different types of objects fell with the same or different rates by experimentally dropping a selection of objects off the Leaning Tower of Pisa; modern experimentalists may measure how energetically small worms in a laboratory are moving around when fed with different dietary patterns (McCloskey *et al.*, 2017) or how many neutrinos pass through a given portion of water in an hour (Spiering, 2020).

The methods used in data analysis to answer scientific questions are, largely, statistical. Statistics is the science of what is probable. Statistical approaches can say what would be expected to occur by chance, and based thereon, it is possible to determine how likely or unlikely a given pattern or observation is, given a set of background assumptions and pre-existing data. In order to assess whether something has just occurred by chance or has an underlying cause, an experiment is typically conducted multiple times, giving a distribution of results. Often, statistical approaches frame the scientific question as a question of whether two series of measurements appear to have been sampled from the same underlying distribution or not. For example, the question whether nurses on average earn the same as teachers is equivalent to the question whether the distribution of salaries of nurses is the same as the distribution of salaries of teachers. Then, if we take a sample from the distribution of salaries of nurses and teachers, for example, by asking some nurses their salary and some teachers theirs, we can use a statistical test to tell us whether the two samples were sampled from identical or different distributions, and thereby whether nurses on average earn the same salaries as teachers.

Statistical approaches to data analysis may certainly appear to be magic to non-statisticians, but they would be unlikely in themselves to be described as artificial intelligence since they involve purely mathematical and rules-driven derivations directly from data, and as discussed in Chapter 1, if it is possible to fully explain a given automatic process, that process is seldom called artificial intelligence, even if it is sophisticated. However, the need for methods derived from the family of approaches that do get called artificial intelligence starts to become clearer when the question involves datasets that are heterogeneous, noisy and unstructured, and where the questions that are being asked are more difficult to formulate in terms of straightforward differences in distributions. Purely statistical methods of data analysis typically require clean and structured data, in which it is possible to compare like with like. In addition, they typically expect clear formulations of the questions that are going to be asked of the data, and that the data satisfies all the required assumptions, such as about the shape of the underlying distribution from which the data are sampled, in order to be able to answer questions with the relevant statistical test. In cases where these requirements are not satisfied, but there is nevertheless a sufficient quantity of representative data that is available to drive learning-based approaches, the methods of artificial intelligence may be adopted for data interpretation.

MAKING DISCOVERIES FROM IMAGES

The previous chapter covered artificial intelligence technologies that work on textual data (from scientific publications) as their input data type. However, in addition to such text, many different data types are involved in scientific discovery: photographs or other images, quantitative measurements such as rainfall levels or blood sugar levels, spectral data, questionnaire responses, sensor measurements, continuous digital tracking of heart rates or activity levels, the quantities of different types of biomolecule in a sample of blood, the amount of electromagnetic radiation falling on a given receiver and more. Each different data item in each different data format provides some information about something. And many of the discoveries we might be interested in are hiding somewhere in these huge volumes of data, and they can only be unearthed if we could just be digitally helped to look in the right places and put the right things together in the right way.

Digital images, in particular, are becoming more widely used in many different aspects of scientific research, due to the relatively low cost of obtaining such images and the high information content they provide. However, depending on what the image is of, many images are inherently challenging to process fully automatically because determining what is in the image requires quite sophisticated and flexible processing. Visual processing fuses together 'lower-level' perceptual functions such as determining areas of light or dark and the borders between them, with higher-level cognitive functions at the same time, such as object recognition and correctly identifying relationships such as inclusion, connection, being above or being next to. For image processing tasks that only require identifying lower-level visual attributes – for example, only detecting the presence of a certain colour or its absence – processing at scale fully automatically requires less algorithmic sophistication. However, image-processing tasks such as object recognition, for example, determining which images are showing trucks as opposed to cars or boats or which images are showing a person taking their dogs for a walk as opposed to being chased by wolves, requires sophisticated algorithmic intelligence (Zhang and Dahu, 2019). And many of the problems in scientific discovery from imaging data require similarly sophisticated algorithmic intelligence and are therefore the subject of intense computational research in support of scientific discovery.

There is perhaps no application area in which imaging has a greater potential for transforming scientific discovery than medical research. Imaging technology is improving our ability to probe and explore aspects of the living human body, from brains to bones and muscles to developing foetuses, in order to detect problems earlier and with greater resolution, and thereby support the development of new treatments and monitor the progress of treatments that are being administered. Some examples of artificial intelligence algorithms that have been developed for the purposes of diagnosing problems from image data include a system that detects retinal diseases based on images taken of the eye (De Fauw *et al.*, 2018) and another system that detects evidence of a stroke having occurred based on images of the brain (Bridge *et al.*, 2022). In most such cases, the systems are trained by being exposed to a manually prepared set of images that have been 'labelled'. That is, the system is trained by being given a large number of images of the relevant type to learn from, in which those that have a condition have been annotated as having the condition, and those that are healthy have been annotated as healthy, and then the system uses this training data to form an internal representation of the differences between images of healthy subjects and images in which the condition is present that it can use to make predictions for images that have not yet been labelled.

A particular challenge in the medical domain is that, depending on the condition and the data type, there may be fewer examples for algorithms to learn from than would be desired. This is partly because many relevant conditions are not extremely common, and then also because it is impossible to share medical data without a robust legal framework for data sharing in which the patient gives consent for their data to be used for downstream research, and agreeing to share their data is not without risks. High-density medical data such as images may surreptitiously 'encode' or reveal additional information about their bearers that could potentially be used against them – such as potential risks of developing other illnesses, for which health insurers might then be unwilling to provide insurance (Yigzaw *et al.*, 2022).

TRANSFER LEARNING

Algorithm developers can use various mitigation strategies in the absence of a large enough and representative enough labelled dataset to use for training purposes. One such approach often used in imaging data is what is known as 'transfer learning'. In this approach, a model is trained in two stages: the model is first trained on a very large dataset that is generally available, and then a subsequent smaller training stage is applied afterward using purpose-built data for a specific problem, with the information that model has learned in the initial stage being 'transferred' to application in the new task. For images, for example, a model might be trained in an initial phase by the model being tasked with predicting back missing 'pixels' or parts of an image taken from a very large image dataset. This pre-training phase results in the model becoming able to apply general rules of how images are put together, such as patterns of light, dark or colours, contours and shapes.

One example of a medical image is the retinal scan. For any given prediction task based on images of this type, the number of examples to learn from is inherently limited. Therefore, when such models are developed, transfer learning may begin first with images from a much larger available collection, such as the ImageNet dataset of 14 million Internet-based images (*ImageNet*, 2022). The same model is then 'fine-tuned' on the target medical image type, retinal scans. This means that the same model, with the parameters already trained on the missing pixel prediction task, is then given the medical image as input and the target prediction as the training task, resulting in the internal parameters of the model being further updated or 'fine-tuned'. Of course, much of what is learned from training a deep learning model to predict missing pixels on images in ImageNet is not directly transferable to the problem of predicting (for example) vascular problems in a retinal scan image. But the basic features of image processing in general, such as detecting borders between different regions or objects in the image, are transferable from one type of image to another. Ideally, when using such a layered approach, the amount of actually labelled data relevant to the problem that you are trying to solve is reduced.

INTERMEDIATE REPRESENTATIONS

When training a complex 'deep' model, what the model learns is a kind of transformation of the input into an internal representation in the form of the weights and parameters associated with the model's processing of the input. This internal representation may in some cases itself be useful for data analysis and interpretation. After all, the model is storing information that was helpful to be able to interpret the images – forming this internal representation can be thought of in broad outline as if the model is searching for meaningful signals in the complexity of the overall image. It makes sense that those signals might sometimes encode meaning in themselves, because of the ability that the model has gained from its training process to self-discover patterns in the data, which can then be used as inputs for further interpretation. This intuition underlies many of the ways in which deep learning models are being used to advance scientific discovery, in the case of imaging data and also in the case of other large and complex unstructured inputs. This unobserved hidden state of the model has a lower dimensionality – it is smaller – than the complex input data. However, because the model is trained to predict missing parts of the data or to make other predictions based on the data, what is represented in these hidden states distills out the most discriminatory and predictive aspects of the input data. For example, in Khojasteh, Aliahmad and Kumar (2018), the internal representation of retinal images learned by a deep neural network was extracted and this representation was subsequently used to predict multiple other clinically relevant phenomena including microaneurysms.

As a further benefit of this kind of representation learning, by transforming diverse types of data into similar representations – sequences of weights in the internal parameter space of a model – these types of learned representations also have the added benefit of allowing different types of data to be interpreted together even when they are structured quite differently. This allows more diverse and complex types of data to be incorporated into scientific investigations, opening up new frontiers of scientific investigation.

DATA, THEORY AND PRIOR KNOWLEDGE

The advent of big data in scientific research has also had its fair share of critics. In particular, there are those who claim that data-driven science, and especially science based on artificial intelligence technologies, neglects theory or leaves theory behind – thus leading some to claim it is 'The End of Theory – the data deluge makes the scientific method obsolete', which is the title of an article in a popular science magazine (Anderson, no date). Scientific activity as it is usually conducted by humans, of course, following the scientific method, makes extensive use of theory in order to formulate hypotheses, design experiments to explore whether those hypotheses hold in particular settings, and integrate the results of experiments. The theory itself is an abstraction from data – the process of theorising involves the formation of generalisations and abstractions from specific examples. It involves forming a model of the way that the world works that both matches the data and has predictive usefulness. Typically, there are multiple possible explanations for any given set of measurements or observations. Forming good theories thus seems to require creativity and intuition, and good theories are therefore both the objective of and the starting point for most scientific discovery research. But in data-driven science, which is sometimes called 'hypothesis-free', it may seem as if all the theorising has disappeared, since the processing operates automatically from the data to the conclusions. Thus, another article in popular media recently asked 'Does the advent of machine learning mean the classic methodology of hypothesise, predict and test has had its day?' (Spinney, 2022)

THE ONGOING NEED FOR THEORY

However, far from being 'the end of theory', theory – and human conceptualisation more generally – permeates all aspects of data analysis and interpretation (Leonelli, 2019), even when analyses are driven by artificial intelligence technologies. To start with, every artificial intelligence system is designed by humans and trained based on objectives set by humans, since there are no artificial intelligence technologies that are capable of deciding on their own learning objectives and selecting their own training data. In this sense, the technical term 'unsupervised learning' as a type of machine learning is misleading, referring as it does to learning to make discriminations in data, in which nevertheless the training objective is still set by humans. In any scientific data-set, some theoretically informed quality criteria have defined what data to gather, what to keep and what to exclude as an outlier or a spoiled measurement, how the quality of the data is assessed and how it is cleaned and which trade-offs are implemented in the associated processing.

Moreover, if labelled data are used in training models, it is theory that defines the vocabulary from which labels are chosen through the choice and definition of keywords or phrases with which to annotate data. It is theory that determines how many labels will be used and specifies the level of detail for the labelling system, which in turn determines which entities will be considered to be essentially the same type of thing and which will be considered distinguishable, with a different identity. Most of the datasets on which models are trained are generated either directly or indirectly by humans, and they are delineated for a particular problem by human selection, informed explicitly or implicitly by theoretical frameworks. And the assessment of the quality of such datasets, as well as the quality and suitability of the associated labelling metadata selection and curation, need to be nuanced and context-specific for the specific problems that the model is being developed to solve.

One particular area in which theory is absolutely essential is in the determination of relationships of cause and effect in a given dataset. Humans understand the world in terms of causes and effects, and often causality is at the heart of the efforts involved in scientific discovery that aim to advance our understanding of the world. But advancing the scientific understanding of causality intrinsically requires theory to be brought together with data. This is because in the absence of a theoretical framework, from data alone it is not possible to infer causal relationships (Pearl, 2018). Causal inference from data requires not only data but also the specification of possible models of what the direction of causal relationships might be, and which factors might be influences or 'moderators' of those relationships (Yao *et al.*, 2020; Schölkopf *et al.*, 2021). To formulate these possibilities and juxtapose the appropriate causal questions with the measured data requires theory.

SIMULATION AS AN AID TO DISCOVERY

Another way in which theoretical knowledge and artificial intelligence systems are converging is in the increasing use of methods that draw from theoretical knowledge and mathematical descriptions of a given system in order to computationally create vast numbers of simulations of different possibilities for answering a given scientific question – and then use data-driven artificial intelligence technologies to explore, process and filter the simulations to select the most likely ones. This type of close-knit interaction between simulation and data-driven science has been hailed by some as a 'fifth paradigm of scientific discovery' ('AI4Science to empower the fifth paradigm of scientific discovery', 2022). The fourth paradigm is already data-driven, but the difference is that the fifth one is anticipated to be based on a combination of empirical data and data generated by the numerical solutions of the fundamental scientific equations themselves, which equations, after all, come from scientific theories, but are hard to solve accurately and at scale.

Training artificial intelligence models with generated data from such equations allows those trained models to function as 'emulators' of the underlying equations themselves, which then can produce predictions in novel scenarios with high efficiency, speeding up the processes involved in this type of research sometimes by several orders of magnitude. This has huge implications in domains where in principle discoveries require enumeration of very large spaces such as the chemical or materials domain – for example, the total number of possible stable materials is thought to be around 10^{180}, or roughly the square of the number of atoms in the known universe. To be able to explore these materials and their properties efficiently within simulation space and then virtually select the ones that are the most promising for actual real-world synthesis is one of the objectives of these forms of theoretically informed simulation and selection-based artificial intelligence technology.

But beyond making use of theory and prior knowledge in these ways, can artificial intelligence technologies guide the creation of new theories? Can they suggest previously unseen variables and interconnections and make coherent advances in our understanding of the world? At least for now, the answer to this question has been negative. Finding the best interpretation of data in the face of a plurality of competing possibilities requires creativity, coherence and intuition – which challenges remain out of reach for automated systems. This makes it notable that an artificial intelligence system was recently used to assist humans in the intuition step in a mathematical discovery process (Davies *et al.*, 2021; Stump, 2021). The authors used an artificial intelligence approach to suggest previously unknown relationships that might be consistent with data and theory, and some of the suggestions were subsequently determined to be accurate and novel discoveries, providing genuine insights into mathematical knot theory and combinatorial theory.

The combination of machine processing capabilities together with human guidance, oversight and selection is a powerful one for accelerating many aspects of scientific discovery. And while data analysis is in a sense restricted to the world of information in which digital algorithms can be expected to operate, the next chapter looks at the ways that these sorts of algorithms can move out into the world itself, into the physical processes that generate data and conduct experiments.

REFERENCES

'AI4Science to empower the fifth paradigm of scientific discovery' (2022) *Microsoft Research*, 7 July. Available at: https://www.microsoft.com/en-us/research/blog/ai4science-to-empower-the-fifth-paradigm-of-scientific-discovery/ (Accessed: 7 July 2022).

AlphaFold Protein Structure Database (2022) Available at: https://alphafold.ebi.ac.uk/ (Accessed: 27 June 2022).

Anderson, C. (no date) 'The end of theory: The data deluge makes the scientific method obsolete', *Wired*. Available at: https://www.wired.com/2008/06/pb-theory/ (Accessed: 12 July 2022).

Bridge, C.P. *et al.* (2022) 'Development and clinical application of a deep learning model to identify acute infarct on magnetic resonance imaging', *Scientific Reports*, 12(1), p. 2154. Available at: https://doi.org/10.1038/s41598-022-06021-0.

Davies, A. *et al.* (2021) 'Advancing mathematics by guiding human intuition with AI', *Nature*, 600(7887), pp. 70–74. Available at: https://doi.org/10.1038/s41586-021-04086-x.

De Fauw, J. *et al.* (2018) 'Clinically applicable deep learning for diagnosis and referral in retinal disease', *Nature Medicine*, 24(9), pp. 1342–1350. Available at: https://doi.org/10.1038/s41591-018-0107-6.

Dill, K.A. *et al.* (2008) 'The protein folding problem', *Annual Review of Biophysics*, 37, pp. 289–316. Available at: https://doi.org/10.1146/annurev.biophys.37.092707.153558.

Hicks, J.L. *et al.* (2019) 'Best practices for analyzing large-scale health data from wearables and smartphone apps', *npj Digital Medicine*, 2(1), pp. 1–12. Available at: https://doi.org/10.1038/s41746-019-0121-1.

ImageNet (2022). Available at: https://www.image-net.org/ (Accessed: 12 July 2022).

Jumper, J. *et al.* (2021) 'Highly accurate protein structure prediction with AlphaFold', *Nature*, pp. 1–11. Available at: https://doi.org/10.1038/s41586-021-03819-2.

Khojasteh, P., Aliahmad, B. and Kumar, D.K. (2018) 'Fundus images analysis using deep features for detection of exudates, hemorrhages and microaneurysms', *BMC Ophthalmology*, 18(1), p. 288. Available at: https://doi.org/10.1186/s12886-018-0954-4.

Kryshtafovych, A., Monastyrskyy, B. and Fidelis, K. (2016) 'CASP11 statistics and the prediction center evaluation system', *Proteins: Structure, Function, and Bioinformatics*, 84(S1), pp. 15–19. Available at: https://doi.org/10.1002/prot.25005.

Lander, E.S. *et al.* (2001) 'Initial sequencing and analysis of the human genome', *Nature*, 409(6822), pp. 860–921. Available at: https://doi.org/10.1038/35057062.

Leonelli, S. (2019) 'The challenges of big data biology', *eLife*, 8, p. e47381. Available at: https://doi.org/10.7554/eLife.47381.

Marx, V. (2013) 'The big challenges of big data', *Nature*, 498(7453), pp. 255–260. Available at: https://doi.org/10.1038/498255a.

McCloskey, R.J. *et al.* (2017) 'Food responsiveness regulates episodic behavioral states in Caenorhabditis elegans', *Journal of Neurophysiology*, 117(5), pp. 1911–1934. Available at: https://doi.org/10.1152/jn.00555.2016.

Pearl, J. (2018) 'Theoretical impediments to machine learning with seven sparks from the causal revolution', *arXiv:1801.04016 [cs, stat]* [Preprint]. Available at: http://arxiv.org/abs/1801.04016 (Accessed: 5 September 2021).

RSCB Protein Data Bank (2022) *PDB statistics: PDB data distribution by experimental method and molecular type*. Available at: https://www.rcsb.org/stats/summary (Accessed: 27 June 2022).

Schölkopf, B. *et al.* (2021) 'Towards causal representation learning', arXiv. Available at: https://doi.org/10.48550/arXiv.2102.11107.

Sebestyén, V., Czvetkó, T. and Abonyi, J. (2021) 'The applicability of big data in climate change research: The importance of system of systems thinking', *Frontiers in Environmental Science*, 9. Available at: https://www.frontiersin.org/article/10.3389/fenvs.2021.619092 (Accessed: 22 June 2022).

Spiering, C. (2020) 'Neutrino Detectors under Water and Ice', in C.W. Fabjan and H. Schopper (eds) *Particle Physics Reference Library: Volume 2: Detectors for Particles and*

Radiation. Cham: Springer International Publishing, pp. 785–822. Available at: https://doi.org/10.1007/978-3-030-35318-6_17.

Spinney, L. (2022) 'Are we witnessing the dawn of post-theory science?', *The Guardian*, 9 January. Available at: https://www.theguardian.com/technology/2022/jan/09/are-we-witnessing-the-dawn-of-post-theory-science (Accessed: 9 January 2022).

Stump, C. (2021) 'Artificial intelligence aids intuition in mathematical discovery', *Nature*, 600(7887), pp. 44–45. Available at: https://doi.org/10.1038/d41586-021-03512-4.

Turbé, H. *et al.* (2021) 'Adaptive time-dependent priors and Bayesian inference to evaluate SARS-CoV-2 public health measures validated on 31 countries', *Frontiers in Public Health*, 8. Available at: https://www.frontiersin.org/article/10.3389/fpubh.2020.583401 (Accessed: 31 March 2022).

Yao, L. *et al.* (2020) 'A survey on causal inference', arXiv. Available at: https://doi.org/10.48550/arXiv.2002.02770.

Yigzaw, K.Y. *et al.* (2022) 'Health Data Security and Privacy: Challenges and Solutions for the Future', in E. Hovenga and H. Grain (eds) *Roadmap to Successful Digital Health Ecosystems*. Academic Press, pp. 335–362. Available at: https://doi.org/10.1016/B978-0-12-823413-6.00014-8.

Zhang, X. and Dahu, W. (2019) 'Application of artificial intelligence algorithms in image processing', *Journal of Visual Communication and Image Representation*, 61, pp. 42–49. Available at: https://doi.org/10.1016/j.jvcir.2019.03.004.

Zhang, Y. and Zhao, Y. (2015) 'Astronomy in the Big Data Era', *Data Science Journal*, 14(0), p. 11. Available at: https://doi.org/10.5334/dsj-2015-011.

4

AI FOR REPRODUCIBLE
RESEARCH

Scientific discoveries happen all the time. Large and small discoveries can occur at any moment, and indeed are taking place right now in laboratories and institutes around the world. They may happen for individuals sitting in front of their computers or microscopes, for teams sitting around a discussion table poring over an interesting photograph, for a research assistant looking at a table of measurement data thinking 'That's strange' or for a professor having just given a presentation in a large auditorium and answering a question from the audience with 'Good question, I don't know the answer – but we'll investigate'. Indeed, scientific discoveries are so common that it could be argued that the hardest part of scientific research is not really the discovery itself. The hard part of scientific research is in proving that a discovery holds up in different contexts and situations and that it reflects something about the world that is intrinsically *repeatable*. After all, it is only through discoveries that are repeatable that we can truly claim to have advanced our collective, cumulative understanding of the world.

This is so for several reasons. First, all science is fallible. Repeating a discovery builds our confidence that we have discovered something about the world that is really true. Second, science is inevitably biased, and each individual and disciplinary perspective is limited.

DOI: 10.1201/9781003226642-4

If a discovery holds up to the different types of scrutiny that different individuals might bring with their different backgrounds or different laboratories with their different micro-environments, then this raises the chances that the finding represents something in the world and not merely an artefact of an individual or disciplinary bias or perspective. Third, we know from history that scientific findings in the past were sometimes overturned by subsequent research. Thus, scientific discoveries may initially be met with scepticism until they have been reproduced in a number of different settings and contexts, by a number of different investigators. It therefore makes more sense to think of scientific discovery not as an individual achievement represented by a single study or a single publication, but as a community-wide slow and evolutionary process in which a body of 'settled science' grows and changes over time through discoveries making their way onto progressively more solid foundations as the volume of research pertaining to them increases.

At least, that is the ideal for the progress of science. In practice, however, across most scientific disciplines, scientific research is facing what is being called a crisis of reproducibility (e.g., Ioannidis, 2005, 2012; Earp and Trafimow, 2015; Munafò et al., 2017; Camerer et al., 2018; Nosek et al., 2021) which detrimentally affects the overall process by which scientific results accumulate. There are several relevant aspects to this crisis. First, across multiple disciplines, many published research findings have failed to replicate in subsequent investigations. Of course, differences in experimental setup and contextual factors may be the reason why some results fail to replicate, and where this is the case, determining what these factors are can lead to more nuanced revisions to our prevailing scientific theories. However, failure to replicate should in most cases reduce our confidence in the robustness and generalisability of the finding.

Additionally, there is systematic evidence of bias in what does get published. Positive results are far more likely to be published, creating an inflated chance of 'false' positive findings among the true positives (Ioannidis, 2005). Statistical 'significance thresholds' are usually used to control the risk of false positive findings but far too many published results have significance only just narrowly above the significance threshold, providing strong evidence for a selection pressure that distorts the true distribution of results. And the source of the selection pressure is not hard to find: all the incentives in scientific research and practice reward discoveries, that is, they reward publications of novel findings (Higginson and Munafò, 2016). However, it is much more difficult to publish negative results or replication efforts leading to disconfirmation of published findings, and even if published these efforts are typically awarded less prestige. It is becoming widely recognised across disciplines that it will be necessary to harness multiple different strategies to improve the reproducibility of scientific research (Munafò et al., 2017), including improvements to statistical and methodological procedures, making separate replication of novel findings a mandatory step in the scientific discovery process, shifting the incentives and default practices in scientific research, and making appropriate use of theory to enable cumulative integration and aggregation across individual studies.

Thus, there is a need for meta-research practices that help to ensure that scientific research is improved to become more reproducible and self-correcting. And various community-led movements are underway in each discipline to direct, energise and bring about these transformations in research practices. But what role is there for artificial intelligence in contributing to these efforts? How can artificial intelligence contribute to the reproducibility of scientific discovery and thereby advance the accumulation of robust findings?

STANDARDISED AND DETAILED REPORTING

One way in which artificial intelligence has the potential to contribute to the reproducibility of scientific research is by assisting with the detailed and standardised reporting of such research. This is because one part of the challenge involved in replicating any pre-existing finding is the difficulties involved in determining what precisely was done at a level of detail sufficient to do exactly the same thing again. This is often not sufficiently well described in the published reports, even though there are guidelines for many different types of research that mandate the level of detail at which methods should be reported (Jin *et al.*, 2018). There are many reasons that published reports might not include enough detail to fully replicate a discovery, but one is that such reports are typically written by humans for humans, and as such, conciseness is a valued attribute. There is clearly a need for different levels of reporting – summary level, as part of a narrative that is pleasant to read within publications, but also full-detail level, for those who wish to attempt replication.

Better reporting can be supported through the digitalisation of scientific discovery, through the adoption of tools that support creating and storing detailed digital records of experiments and procedures that then form a part of the overall digital record underpinning a discovery and enhancing its replicability (Gerlach, Untucht and Stefan, 2020) – in formats that are searchable and archivable, and keep track of the associated data as well as the procedures that were performed in ways that ease their subsequent rediscovery (Willoughby and Frey, 2022). Standards for the description of entities and experimental procedures are a key component of the effort towards better reporting.

SCIENTIFIC ONTOLOGIES FOR STANDARDISED REPORTING

Scientific ontologies are standardised computable representations of the entities that are the subject matter of scientific investigations in a given domain (Hastings, 2017). They are built on the basis of the logical technologies for knowledge representation and automated reasoning, which formed the foundations for the first wave of artificial intelligence technologies – expert systems. However, although technologies for automated reasoning are still used in the maintenance and application of these knowledge-rich domain representations, it is their use as a standard that underscores their contribution to better reporting. Scientific ontologies exist for many different subject matters across many different scientific disciplines, from chemistry (Hastings *et al.*, 2016) and biology (The Gene Ontology Consortium, 2019) to behavioural science (Michie *et al.*, 2020), psychology (Larsen and Hastings, 2018) and medicine (Bodenreider, Cornet and Vreeman, 2018).

A key feature of scientific ontologies when used to facilitate scientific integration is that they include not just a representation of types or broad groupings of kinds of entity (such as molecule, gene, behaviour and emotion) but also a detailed representation of, and hierarchical arrangement of, the entities at the level of detail that features in scientific investigations (e.g., 'L-dopamine', 'BRCA1', 'solar radiation receiver' and 'happiness'). Having a semantic, defined, annotated and hierarchically arranged index for the entities that feature in scientific investigations enables data about such entities to be integrated across studies and aggregated flexibly and dynamically. The ways in which ontologies contribute to the scientific discovery process are diverse, including providing the vocabularies for indexes of experimental descriptions, literature resources and data, providing a hierarchy that can be used to aggregate findings, allowing 'zooming' in and out of levels of detail, and supporting the development of artificial intelligence technologies to provide an automated summary and detail-level views on the same information (Haendel, Chute and Robinson, 2018).

An ontology creates a shared terminology and way of classifying things in a scientific domain. Therefore, it needs to be flexible enough to represent the full breadth of research in the domain, as well as remain extensible, as new entities are regularly suggested in the course of ongoing scientific research. The ontology can serve as a track record of the evolution of the theoretical thinking of an entire community, linking entities to a history of relevant discoveries. By serving as a 'knowledge hub' for a scientific community, an ontology-organised knowledge base provides a view across the whole of what is known in a given field, an integrated synthesis of the available evidence. And the association of detailed computable ontologies with experimental descriptions increases the reproducibility of scientific investigations (Willoughby and Frey, 2022).

But keeping track of every detail of every scientific process, and associating those details with computable descriptions drawn from scientific ontologies, takes time and effort. And, in some sense, it is punishing work – repetitive and frustrating. Therefore, it is a primary candidate for support from artificial intelligence technologies. To what extent can keeping detailed, accurate, and reproducible information about experimental descriptions and associated data be automated by intelligent systems?

AUTOMATING EXPERIMENTAL DESCRIPTIONS

One direction that is being explored in support of the digitalisation of the descriptions of scientific processes, involves the use of artificial intelligence algorithms to create formal digital descriptions from handwritten laboratory notebooks (Memon et al., 2020), which were the traditional way that experimental processes and results were documented in scientific investigations – with accompanying idiosyncratic handwriting and style unique to each scientist, and not digitally searchable or retrievable. Being able to automatically convert handwriting to digital text is clearly a challenging task for machine intelligence – handwriting differs from person to person, from language to language, and even from page to page. For optimal performance, a machine learning system needs to be trained specifically for the writing of an individual. However, systems that are trained on examples of writing from multiple individuals do show reasonably good performance – with accuracies of determining handwritten letters of above 90% and up to 98% across many languages (Akouaydi et al., 2019). However, scientific text in laboratory notebooks poses particular challenges for the translation of handwriting into digital text, as such notebooks are liable to include many idiosyncratic abbreviations and technical terms. Thus, there is ample room for further research to advance algorithms to learn over time to recognise individual patterns of writing and expression. Similarly, another avenue by which artificial intelligence technology has the potential to make the capture of detailed experimental descriptions easier is speech recognition technology which converts spoken words to written text automatically (Aldarmaki *et al.*, 2022). And even once experimental descriptions have been digitalised, management, governance and documentation of associated data and electronic descriptions of discovery processes are essential to ensure their full value is retained into the future (Willoughby and Frey, 2022).

AUTOMATING DATA ANNOTATION AND SHARING

Ideally, the data underlying a scientific discovery should be available to be directly validated or re-used in subsequent research, as far as is allowable given the nature of the underlying data and respecting the privacy of any human participants. However, this ideal is frequently not achieved in practice (Gabelica, Bojčić and Puljak, 2022). Advances in the comprehensiveness and scope of the data available via open data resources will directly advance scientific research, results and practice as well as reduce the opportunities for media reports to stand in isolation, as such databases provide a background into which novel findings can be integrated and synthesised. In the previous chapter, we saw an example of a scientific innovation that depended on the open availability of scientific data – the AlphaFold protein structure prediction algorithm which was trained on vast quantities of open and well-annotated public biological data.

Scientific ontologies are used to carefully annotate data across databases in large part by the careful and meticulous work of human experts. Human resources for this type of data management are always limited; thus, innovation in the ways in which data 'curation' takes place has the potential to have significant downstream cumulative effects. Typically, the tools that support this work are custom-built for each data type, database and group. Although a few cross-domain tools do exist, they are not yet widely adopted.

The potential for artificial intelligence approaches to support the process of data management is enormous, by automatically predicting standardised labels and associated descriptions for data items. Although in most domains, results for fully automated curation pipelines are not yet sufficiently reliable and generalisable to be able to entirely replace human expertise, there are approaches that support human curation by pre-preparing content, and aiding in filtering, retrieval and organisation (Bileschi et al., 2022; Glauer et al., 2022). These ensure that the effort of the human is used as efficiently as possible, as well as ensuring robust and comprehensive information flows between different producers and platforms.

Artificial intelligence technologies may also contribute to virtuous feedback cycles of data improvement by highlighting data quality issues. They can do this by the iterative application of cycles of prediction and estimation, in which the confidence of a prediction that a model generates is then associated in reverse with the quality of subsets of the input data. That is, lower quality predictions are associated with lower quality input data. This association then allows potentially problematic data records to be identified and corrected, in an approach that has been termed 'data-centric AI' (Press, no date; *Why it's time for 'data-centric artificial intelligence'*, no date).

Thus far, we have surveyed approaches by which artificial intelligence technologies support the digitalisation and standardisation of data, including formal descriptions of experiments. Once experiments have been formally described in a computable form, they are then themselves available for algorithms to operate on. Another exciting potential for support from automation is opened up by virtue of the availability of digital experimental descriptions: artificial intelligence-assisted experimental design.

ARTIFICIALLY LEARNING EXPERIMENTAL DESIGN

A frontier application area for the use of algorithms to help in the design of experiments is chemical synthesis and process design. In chemical reactions, input molecules are transformed into output molecules via chemical reactions that rearrange atoms and bonds.

The structural variety of possible chemical entities is unimaginably huge (Reymond, 2015), and their potential reactions are also a massive combinatorial space. Reaction process design typically involves exploring this potential combinatorial space of possibilities towards a specific outcome (e.g., molecules to be synthesised from specified precursors) while taking into consideration some criteria to be optimised (Eyke, Green and Jensen, 2020). Once again, sophisticated data description underlies the possibility for algorithmic processes to learn to design experiments, of which a good example is a recently released comprehensive and computable chemical synthesis database (Rohrbach *et al.*, 2022). However, the process by which experiments are designed is also an interesting frontier for artificial intelligence technologies, in part because it requires a different type of algorithm.

The exploration of possible (hypothetical) reaction chains – chains of reaction processes in which the outputs of one process form the inputs to the next process in the chain – to generate desired outputs involves a combinatorial explosion of possibilities, each of which involves uncertainty, so that the final results, accumulating uncertainties, are not really knowable even with a brute force approach to enumerate all the possibilities algorithmically. To navigate this huge combinatorial space thus requires a different approach which is able to reduce uncertainty in a targeted way until the final result becomes more predictable. This family of algorithmic approaches is known as active learning: processes in which a predictive model is iteratively updated based on results of experiments that were themselves selected to be maximally informative on the basis of the results of a prior iteration of the model. Active learning algorithms are able to predict which experiments would be maximally informative for reducing the uncertainties in the predictions the model is able to make. Those experiments may then be conducted in a targeted fashion, and the results fed back into the learning model which again predicts the outcomes and highlights the predictions that are maximally informative. This iterative algorithmically assisted process allows for the determination of optimal reaction designs without having to exhaustively test all possible combinations. For example, DeepReact+ is an active learning tool for chemical reaction outcome prediction for use in planning chemical syntheses (Gong *et al.*, 2021).

Active learning has also been used in the science of discovering new materials with optimal properties for some objective (Lookman *et al.*, 2019). The discovery – or rather, design – of new materials with desirable properties is one of the scientific areas with the greatest potential for revolutionising the future. Materials that are stronger, lighter and more resistant to environmental damages can lead to better, longer-lasting and more energy-efficient equipment, clothing, transportation options and even houses. Like the general problem of designing chemical reactions to produce specific chemicals, materials design is combinatorial – materials are built up from parts – and it is not feasible to conduct all the experiments that might be needed in order to reduce the uncertainty involved in designing novel materials with desirable properties. Thus, active learning is used iteratively in materials design for desirable properties, starting from what is known and the desired outcome to be optimised, to select the experiments which will in turn be used to narrow the search space and augment the training data for the subsequent iteration. Some examples where this strategy has been used to drive accelerated discoveries include the discovery of new 'shape memory alloys' (Xue *et al.*, 2016), which are metals that can be bent or stretched when cool but then return to their original shape on heating, and the design of LEDs to maximise light emission efficiencies (Rouet-Leduc *et al.*, 2016).

In addition to materials design, artificial intelligence-driven optimisation can be used to design biomolecular engines that have the potential to act in ways that address challenges in environmental management, or that produce biological substances at scale. Enzymes are the active proteins that catalyse chemical reactions in living systems, and the full range and complexity of enzymatic diversity in ecosystems are staggering. Without enzymatic catalysts, most of the metabolic and tissue maintenance chemical reaction processes underlying life would not be possible. Thus, one of the most exciting frontiers for the design of new and desirable reactions is the engineering of novel enzymes able to catalyse such reactions. For an example of the application of artificial intelligence technology to this discovery frontier, artificial intelligence has been used to guide the engineering of novel enzymes able to degrade plastic in the environment (Lu *et al.*, 2022). As plastics are not naturally degradable by existing living organisms in the ecosystems that they are now polluting, engineering artificial enzymes that are able to degrade them is an important scientific target. However, engineered enzymes tend not to be stable at a range of pHs and temperatures, which means they might work in a controlled laboratory environment but not in practice where they are needed to degrade environmental pollutants. The artificial intelligence algorithm was used to identify stabilising mutations for different pHs and temperature ranges in order to guide the optimal design of engineered enzymes for both function and stability.

RESEARCH PROCESS AUTOMATION

One of the most powerful ways that digitalisation and the development of associated technologies are changing scientific discovery is through the automation of scientific experiments (Ford and McElvania, 2020). Automation addresses challenges that arise due to human error, addresses fatigue and under-resourcing in discovery research and allows scaling up discovery massively. Best of all, the types of experimental processes that are amenable to automation are typically those that are the least interesting for humans to perform, freeing up time for humans to do the more fun parts of the discovery process, such as staring at data and having 'a-ha!' moments.

The vision of a robot scientist, endowed by advances in robotics and artificial intelligence with the physical and mental capability to independently conduct research tasks (at least within a narrowly constrained domain), is a compelling one that has long captured the minds of researchers. Two prototypes of such robot scientist systems, named Adam and Eve, are described in (Sparkes *et al.*, 2010).

These systems each consist of a robotic unit designed to operate within a modified laboratory environment, controlled by custom software. Adam was able to conduct laboratory investigations into the genes underlying the metabolic pathways of yeast, a common organism used for the study of metabolism as a 'closed loop' or an autonomous system, while Eve was able to perform high-throughput screening for potential new drugs. The success of these prototype systems depended on the comprehensive formal and computable description of each step in the associated scientific investigations in order to transform each step into actions that could be automated. Adam and Eve use computational models of their objects of investigation together with machine-reasoning processes to collect and interpret experimental results.

Adam and Eve were robotic systems that operated on fixed tracks, without the freedom to move around the laboratory aside from along their narrowly constrained tracks. More recently, a robot was developed to assist in materials discovery that was able to roam freely around the laboratory environment in order to conduct experiments and was even able to select experiments to perform (from amongst a narrow set of choices), while avoiding getting in the way of any human experimenters sharing the same lab space (Burger et al., 2020). This mobile robotic chemist used a combination of laser scanning and touch feedback to locate itself and move freely within a standardised laboratory environment – therefore being able to operate even in complete darkness if needed for performing light-sensitive experiments, which are usually challenging for humans to perform. It is battery-driven and therefore needs recharging, but can work for more than 21 hours per day around the requirement for charging time. Artificial intelligence algorithms are used to guide the performance of the experiments by the robot. It was estimated that this robot, armed with the ability to perform experiments in a customisable and high-throughput fashion, was able to reduce the time it took to make discoveries in the laboratory from months to mere days. However, the authors admit that the design of the workflow that allowed the robot to achieve this objective took years – and that the robot's algorithms are not (yet) transferable to alternative application domains.

A full vision of automation for the scientific research laboratory of the future, assisted by artificial intelligence, must encompass not only robotic actors who are able to perform experiments analogously to how humans perform experiments but also smart devices more generally, powered by sensor technologies. This vision has been called a 'self-driving' laboratory (Butakova *et al.*, 2022), in which not only the experiments and their interpretation are automated but so too are the background functions needed for a fully functional environment, such as waste disposal. However, aside from smaller targeted scenarios such as reported by Rooney *et al.* (2022) for the discovery of novel adhesives, this grand vision has not yet been actualised in practice in a general laboratory setting, and it is likely to be achieved only incrementally in an application-specific way.

AUTOMATION AND JOB LOSS

No discussion of the role of artificial intelligence technologies in advancing automation in any domain would be complete without reference to the fear that such automation will inevitably lead to the loss of jobs for humans (Acemoglu and Restrepo, 2018). Employment opportunities are vital to the healthy and sustainable functioning of any society, both in terms of the happiness and fulfillment of individuals and in terms of the overall economic engine by which money is circulated to the population and businesses. If there are more jobs taken by automated agents, and if that leads to there being fewer jobs available for humans, then while the profit margins might increase for the organisations that use such automation – or in our application scenario, the cost of conducting scientific research might decrease – there will nevertheless be more unemployed people who are not able to productively contribute to the economy. Scientific research is a significant employer in most modern countries with large economies. Thus, there is a real risk if the potential for auto-mation becomes too all-encompassing, and may require redesigned economic systems in order to mitigate the negative societal effects that might transpire accordingly.

However, the history of job loss due to automation that has happened so far has taught us not to be too worried about this potential future scenario. This is because the types of processes that are amenable to automation – and the types of robots that we are able to create accordingly to perform those tasks – tend to be simple, repetitive processes, while the types of work required by a typical employment scenario are diverse and require genuine human intelligence, social awareness, and varied capacities for fine motor control – trained by millions of years of evolution – for which technology has still got a long way to go (if ever) before it catches up.

Ultimately, scientific discovery involves all the processes involved in the generation and interpretation of data to answer questions. Importantly, scientific discovery is not merely a process that progresses linearly from identified problems or questions to determined solutions. The process also involves problem formulation – and problem selection (*A first lesson in meta-rationality* | *Meta-rationality*, 2016). These latter are much harder to automate than the former. The skills of meta-rationality and adaptive reasoning are needed in order to do science well – being able to shift perspective, reformulate a problem, shift the foundations for the question you are trying to answer. And to think of new questions at all. For the foreseeable future, it is most likely that artificial intelligence-driven advances in automation in scientific discovery will need to progress alongside and operate in support of human efforts, rather than replacing humans. But are the technologies that we have available at the moment achieving their full potential, and are they up to the tasks that are being set for them in the context of scientific discovery? These questions may be illuminated by the discussions in the next chapter.

REFERENCES

A first lesson in meta-rationality | *Meta-rationality* (2016) Available at: https://metarationality.com/bongard-meta-rationality (Accessed: 27 June 2022).

Acemoglu, D. and Restrepo, P. (2018) 'Artificial intelligence, automation and work', National Bureau of Economic Research, p. 43. Available at: https://doi.org/10.3386/w24196.

Akouaydi, H. *et al.* (2019) 'Neural architecture based on fuzzy perceptual representation for online multilingual handwriting recognition'. arXiv. Available at: https://doi.org/10.48550/arXiv.1908.00634.

Aldarmaki, H. *et al.* (2022) 'Unsupervised automatic speech recognition: A review', *Speech Communication*, 139, pp. 76–91. Available at: https://doi.org/10.1016/j.specom.2022.02.005.

Bileschi, M.L. *et al.* (2022) 'Using deep learning to annotate the protein universe', *Nature Biotechnology*, 40(6), pp. 932–937. Available at: https://doi.org/10.1038/s41587-021-01179-w.

Bodenreider, O., Cornet, R. and Vreeman, D.J. (2018) 'Recent developments in clinical terminologies - SNOMED CT, LOINC, and RxNorm', *Yearbook of Medical Informatics*, 27(1), pp. 129–139. Available at: https://doi.org/10.1055/s-0038-1667077.

Burger, B. *et al.* (2020) 'A mobile robotic chemist', *Nature*, 583(7815), pp. 237–241. Available at: https://doi.org/10.1038/s41586-020-2442-2.

Butakova, M.A. *et al.* (2022) 'Data-centric architecture for self-driving laboratories with autonomous discovery of new nanomaterials', *Nanomaterials*, 12(1), p. 12. Available at: https://doi.org/10.3390/nano12010012.

Camerer, C.F. *et al.* (2018) 'Evaluating the replicability of social science experiments in nature and science between 2010 and 2015', *Nature Human Behaviour*, 2(9), pp. 637–644. Available at: https://doi.org/10.1038/s41562-018-0399-z.

Earp, B.D. and Trafimow, D. (2015) 'Replication, falsification, and the crisis of confidence in social psychology', *Frontiers in Psychology*, 6. Available at: https://doi.org/10.3389/fpsyg.2015.00621.

Eyke, N.S., Green, W.H. and Jensen, K.F. (2020) 'Iterative experimental design based on active machine learning reduces the experimental burden associated with reaction screening', *Reaction Chemistry & Engineering*, 5(10), pp. 1963–1972. Available at: https://doi.org/10.1039/D0RE00232A.

Ford, B.A. and McElvania, E. (2020) 'Machine learning takes laboratory automation to the next level', *Journal of Clinical Microbiology*, 58(4), pp. e00012–e00020. Available at: https://doi.org/10.1128/JCM.00012-20.

Gabelica, M., Bojčić, R. and Puljak, L. (2022) 'Many researchers were not compliant with their published data sharing statement: Mixed-methods study', *Journal of Clinical Epidemiology*, pp. 33–41. Available at: https://doi.org/10.1016/j.jclinepi.2022.05.019.

Gerlach, B., Untucht, C. and Stefan, A. (2020) 'Electronic Lab Notebooks and Experimental Design Assistants', in A. Bespalov, M.C. Michel, and T. Steckler (eds) *Good Research Practice in Non-Clinical Pharmacology and Biomedicine*. Cham: Springer International Publishing (Handbook of Experimental Pharmacology), pp. 257–275. Available at: https://doi.org/10.1007/164_2019_287.

Glauer, M. *et al.* (2022) 'Interpretable ontology extension in chemistry', *Semantic Web Journal* [Preprint]. Available at: https://doi.org/10.5281/ZENODO.6023497.

Gong, Y. *et al.* (2021) 'DeepReac+: Deep active learning for quantitative modeling of organic chemical reactions', *Chemical Science*, 12(43), pp. 14459–14472. Available at: https://doi.org/10.1039/D1SC02087K.

Haendel, M.A., Chute, C.G. and Robinson, P.N. (2018) 'Classification, ontology, and precision medicine', *New England Journal of Medicine*, 379(15), pp. 1452–1462. Available at: https://doi.org/10.1056/NEJMra1615014.

Hastings, J. (2017) 'Primer on Ontologies', in C. Dessimoz and N. Škunca (eds) *The Gene Ontology Handbook*. New York, NY: Springer New York (Methods in Molecular Biology), pp. 3–13. Available at: https://doi.org/10.1007/978-1-4939-3743-1_1.

Hastings, J. *et al.* (2016) 'ChEBI in 2016: Improved services and an expanding collection of metabolites', *Nucleic Acids Research*, 44(D1), pp. D1214–D1219. Available at: https://doi.org/10.1093/nar/gkv1031.

Higginson, A.D. and Munafò, M.R. (2016) 'Current incentives for scientists lead to underpowered studies with erroneous conclusions', *PLOS Biology*, 14(11), p. e2000995. Available at: https://doi.org/10.1371/journal.pbio.2000995.

Ioannidis, J.P.A. (2005) 'Why most published research findings are false', *PLoS Medicine*, 2(8), p. e124. Available at: https://doi.org/10.1371/journal.pmed.0020124.

Ioannidis, J.P.A. (2012) 'Why science is not necessarily self-correcting', *Perspectives on Psychological Science*, 7(6), pp. 645–654. Available at: https://doi.org/10.1177/1745691612464056.

Jin, Y. *et al.* (2018) 'Does the medical literature remain inadequately described despite having reporting guidelines for 21 years? – A systematic review of reviews: An update', *Journal of Multidisciplinary Healthcare*, 11, pp. 495–510. Available at: https://doi.org/10.2147/JMDH.S155103.

Larsen, R.R. and Hastings, J. (2018) 'From affective science to psychiatric disorder: Ontology as a semantic bridge', *Frontiers in Psychiatry*, 9(487), pp. 1–13. Available at: https://doi.org/10.3389/fpsyt.2018.00487.

Lookman, T. *et al.* (2019) 'Active learning in materials science with emphasis on adaptive sampling using uncertainties for targeted design', *npj Computational Materials*, 5(1), pp. 1–17. Available at: https://doi.org/10.1038/s41524-019-0153-8.

Lu, H. *et al.* (2022) 'Machine learning-aided engineering of hydrolases for PET depolymerization', *Nature*, 604(7907), pp. 662–667. Available at: https://doi.org/10.1038/s41586-022-04599-z.

Memon, J. *et al.* (2020) 'Handwritten optical character recognition (OCR): A comprehensive systematic literature review (SLR)', *IEEE Access*, 8, pp. 142642–142668. Available at: https://doi.org/10.1109/ACCESS.2020.3012542.

Michie, S. *et al.* (2020) 'Representation of behaviour change interventions and their evaluation: Development of the upper level of the behaviour change intervention ontology', *Wellcome Open Research*, 5, p. 123. Available at: https://doi.org/10.12688/wellcomeopenres.15902.1.

Munafò, M.R. *et al.* (2017) 'A manifesto for reproducible science', *Nature Human Behaviour*, 1(1), p. 0021. Available at: https://doi.org/10.1038/s41562-016-0021.

Nosek, B.A. *et al.* (2021) *Replicability, robustness, and reproducibility in psychological science*, PsyArXiv. Available at: https://doi.org/10.31234/osf.io/ksfvq.

Press, G. (no date) *Andrew Ng Launches A Campaign For Data-Centric AI*, Forbes. Available at: https://www.forbes.com/sites/gilpress/2021/06/16/andrew-ng-launches-a-campaign-for-data-centric-ai/ (Accessed: 23 June 2021).

Reymond, J.-L. (2015) 'The chemical space project', *Accounts of Chemical Research*, 48(3), pp. 722–730. Available at: https://doi.org/10.1021/ar500432k.

Rohrbach, S. *et al.* (2022) 'Digitization and validation of a chemical synthesis literature database in the ChemPU', *Science*, 377(6602), pp. 172–180. Available at: https://doi.org/10.1126/science.abo0058.

Rooney, M.B. *et al.* (2022) 'A self-driving laboratory designed to accelerate the discovery of adhesive materials', *Digital Discovery* [Preprint]. Available at: https://doi.org/10.1039/D2DD00029F.

Rouet-Leduc, B. *et al.* (2016) 'Optimisation of GaN LEDs and the reduction of efficiency droop using active machine learning', *Scientific Reports*, 6(1), p. 24862. Available at: https://doi.org/10.1038/srep24862.

Sparkes, A. *et al.* (2010) 'Towards Robot Scientists for autonomous scientific discovery', *Automated Experimentation*, 2(1), p. 1. Available at: https://doi.org/10.1186/1759-4499-2-1.

The Gene Ontology Consortium (2019) 'The gene ontology resource: 20 years and still going strong', *Nucleic Acids Research*, 47(D1), pp. D330–D338. Available at: https://doi.org/10.1093/nar/gky1055.

Why it's time for 'data-centric artificial intelligence' (no date) MIT Sloan. Available at: https://mitsloan.mit.edu/ideas-made-to-matter/why-its-time-data-centric-artificial-intelligence (Accessed: 10 October 2022).

Willoughby, C. and Frey, J.G. (2022) 'Data management matters', *Digital Discovery*, 1(3), pp. 183–194. Available at: https://doi.org/10.1039/D1DD00046B.

Xue, Dezhen *et al.* (2016) 'Accelerated search for materials with targeted properties by adaptive design', *Nature Communications*, 7(1), p. 11241. Available at: https://doi.org/10.1038/ncomms11241.

5

LIMITATIONS OF AI
AND STRATEGIES FOR
COMBATING BIAS

Throughout the 70-year-long history of the development of artificial intelligence technologies, promises have been made and broken. Early artificial intelligence researchers thought that problems
such as computer vision, language understanding, and general
human intelligence would be solvable within a single generation.
But, such tantalising visions of future breakthroughs that seemed
just around the corner have been routinely followed by disappoint-
ments, as the complexity of the challenges involved became clearer.
Part of the reason for this hope-hype-bust cycle is surely that as
humans, we don't really understand ourselves, thus, in attempting
to design machines in our own image, we have at times had too
little information to go by. Even in very simple organisms such as
flies and worms, the basis of intelligence is not well understood –
and our scientific understanding of the basis of human intelligence
is still in some sense only in its infancy.

At the same time, even while our detailed scientific understanding of human intelligence is limited, our intuitive understanding of
ordinary human capabilities is quite sophisticated, even if largely
driven by intuition and projection. Indeed, as a social species we
appear to be rather eager to project human traits and inferences

DOI: 10.1201/9781003226642-5

from our own inner cognitive experience onto all the things in our environment, including other humans, where it is justified, but also our pets, and even inanimate objects at times. With artificial intelligence algorithms, we are literally designing them to deliberately mimic human intelligence, in a sense, they are being designed to 'fool' humans. Is it any wonder that we talk about such systems as if they possessed human capabilities? Where do the projections end and the true nature of machine intelligence begin? And what is the implication for scientific discovery?

The COVID pandemic has been in many ways a success story for scientific discovery. The sequence of the virus, the symptoms, and the ways in which the virus spread were mapped out by researchers in record time and shared globally, which helped countries to prepare and respond to the crisis as it unfolded. The vaccines that were developed to combat the virus and thereby save lives used new mRNA vaccine technologies that were the result of many years of careful and cumulative preparatory scientific discovery, which came together at the right moment to bring vaccines to the market in record time. However, the pandemic also brought into the societal spotlight several challenges and risks relating to information technologies, artificial intelligence and the general advance of automation in all aspects of our human lives.

THE ROLE OF ARTIFICIAL INTELLIGENCE IN THE MISINFORMATION 'INFODEMIC'

The pandemic, along with other geopolitical events of the last decade, has shown just how severe the real-world consequences can be for the spread of incorrect information or 'fake news' (Lazer *et al.*, 2018; Scheufele and Krause, 2019; Yeung *et al.*, 2021). The problem of rapidly spreading misinformation – and disinformation, or misinformation that is deliberately created and spread – is exacerbated when the information in question is scientific, as scientific information serves as the basis on which people form beliefs about actions to take that potentially affect societal cohesion, population health outcomes or political stability. In the terminology of a report on the topic that was published in the early stages of the pandemic in the scientific journal *Nature*, the battle against COVID-related misinformation and conspiracy theories was (and remains) of 'epic' proportions (Ball and Maxmen, 2020), necessitating coordinated action on all fronts. The World Health Organisation has repeatedly issued warnings about an 'infodemic' of scientific and health-related misinformation. The result is a paradox: at the time when scientific achievements are growing at a staggering pace, the level of trust in science – and in scientific expertise – is dropping.

Misinformation affects all disciplines, although it may be particularly problematic for health-related information (Wang *et al.*, 2019), with a case in point being the engineered controversy surrounding vaccination and the resulting fall in vaccination uptake – and resurgence of disease – throughout the developed world (Browne, 2018) (even prior to the start of the COVID-19 pandemic). New media technologies such as globalised social media platforms, driven by artificial intelligence algorithms which filter, select and amplify units of information algorithmically, are thought to play a key role as they enable ultra-rapid transmission of any kind of information regardless of its veracity. Indeed, some studies have suggested that misinformation may spread faster on these platforms and reach a wider audience than accurate information (Vosoughi, Roy and Aral, 2018), due to an underlying attribute that might be called something like information 'infectiousness' (Juul and Ugander, 2021). It has proven very difficult to make algorithms able to robustly discern accurate from inaccurate content, which objective remains a challenge even for humans that are trained as fact-checkers.

Algorithms amplify the transmission of information according to the patterns of what users have previously liked and shared, to show users more of the same type of content that they will be anticipated to then also like and share. This means that users who have liked and shared content with a given theme tend to be shown more content that fits that theme, and less content that challenges those ideas, creating 'echo chambers' of self-similar beliefs and messages (Cinelli *et al.*, 2021). These echo chambers are antagonistic to the discourses and exchanges between different perspectives that help to build societal cohesion and keep communities safe. Another challenge is that new media platforms may have algorithmic (fake) participants – bots – liking, commenting and sharing content with the explicit objective that the content they are targeting gets amplified since the underlying algorithms depend on the popularity of the content and the bots are able to algorithmically make certain content appear more popular. For the limited types of 'conversation' that take place on social media, it can be difficult to robustly recognise the genuinely human participants from the algorithmic participants.

Proposed solutions to the infodemic emphasise fact-checking and 'inoculation' (e.g., van der Linden *et al.*, 2017; Roozenbeek and van der Linden, 2019), a process in which users of new media technologies are trained to fact-check content before they share it. The importance of scientists themselves participating in these media platforms and actively countering misinformation has also been emphasised (Iyengar and Massey, 2019). However, the problem of misinformation about science is not just a problem of new media technologies – nor of public awareness (Wynne, 2006). It is a problem that has grown against a background in which science itself is facing several transformative challenges including that of reproducibility as discussed in the previous chapter, and it is partly reflective of those challenges.

Scientific research takes place against a backdrop of incentives, practices and cultures in which research career success and cumulative scientific progress are not always aligned (Higginson and Munafò, 2016), and isolated and implausible findings may be favoured over robust, cumulative and repeatable research. Moreover, there are many institutional and disciplinary incentives for scientific research to be represented in an exaggerated form in media reports. The general public is thus ordinarily exposed to an endless series of contradictory, weakly supported findings being over-reported in the media. The result is an appearance of fragmentation within the scientific community over and above the discourses, debates and differences that are a normal part of the scientific process. The appearance of radical fragmentation combined with algorithmic amplification exacerbates the problem of misinformation. Is it any wonder that the general public learns to distrust scientific findings and then tries to evaluate for themselves what is true and what is false, even in topics for which they lack the needed expertise to make a fully informed evaluation, resulting in vulnerabilities to targeted disinformation?

To reduce the appearance of fragmentation, there is a need to move beyond reporting isolated research findings towards presenting research findings in the context of a comprehensive and integrated body of evolving evidence to which individual findings contribute, but which is continuously updated. It is necessary, but not sufficient, to make data available and open because a flood of unintegrated and uninterpreted data is overwhelming and only accessible to those who already have the expertise to process and integrate such datasets. Intelligent and continuous integration is needed in order to link data to theory and conclusions and provide overviews and summaries that represent the scientific findings as a whole in a way that is accessible to all consumers, including those who are not experts in that field. Integration and summarisation will reduce the appearance of contradiction in the resulting evidence base: in neuroscience, for example, differences in analytical workflows have been shown to lead to differences in results even on the same dataset (Botvinik-Nezer, 2020), however, meta-analyses across the different results converged on a consensus.

The ability to meaningfully aggregate across studies and to grow the background against which surprising findings are tested is key to the progress of science as a whole. Due to the volumes of evidence, this creates a need for algorithmic support from artificial intelligence in support of a more holistic approach to evidence generation and integration. The background of robust and integrated evidence would then be able to act as a safeguard against the danger of algorithmic amplification of disinformation.

But to achieve these objectives will require algorithms that do not have unexpected outcomes or side effects. Some of the harms that arise potentially and in practice from the implementation of artificial intelligence algorithms relate more directly to the question of how robust and reliable we are able to make such systems. Are we able to make algorithms that really work?

ARTIFICIAL INTELLIGENCE IS EVERYWHERE, BUT DOES IT WORK?

Arriving, as it did, in the wake of an explosion in the development and implementation of artificial intelligence algorithms throughout the previous decade, the COVID pandemic was an opportunity for such algorithms to show their value when applied to a rapidly evolving and novel global challenge. Could artificial intelligence be used to pave the way to better diagnosis, prognosis and therapeutics for the novel virus?

One objective in the early stages of the pandemic, for example, was to detect COVID from clinical standard-of-care images, such as chest radiographs and computed tomography images. And as such, during the first year of the pandemic, a great number of artificial intelligence systems that aimed to address this task were trained on data from the early stages of the outbreak. These systems appeared to show good results and were accordingly published. However, in a subsequent systematic review, *none of them* were found to be usable in practice in a clinical setting (Roberts *et al.*, 2021). In other words, even though they scored well on the benchmarks which are used to evaluate such models for the purposes of publication, they didn't really 'work' in practice in the setting in which they should have been useful. It is worth considering the reasons identified for why these models failed to translate into practical usability, as they can serve as general guidance for the pitfalls in the development and evaluation of artificial intelligence systems.

Firstly, over two thirds of the published models did not complete any external validation. Internal validation is when the same data source as is used in creating the model is also used in the testing of the model, which is the usual starting point for evaluation. In a robust internal validation, the available data is usually split into a training portion used to develop the model and a testing portion used to evaluate the model. External validation, which involves testing the model on an external dataset that was not used at all in the model's development, provides a very important test for the model's generalisability – an indicator of how the model might work in practice on new data that would be obtained after the model is deployed, and on which the model would be making genuine predictions. Nor did most of the studies complete any prospective evaluation – evaluation on data that is newly collected after the model has been developed – on outcomes that matter.

External and prospective validation are both essential ingredients that reflect the importance of checking how an artificial intelligence system performs the actual task that it has been designed to perform in the context which it is intended to be deployed, rather than just its performance on any intermediary or proxy tasks, no matter how similar the proxy task is believed to be to the actual task. The differences between the proxy context and the real-life context for the operation of the system may appear to be trivial from a theoretical perspective, but failing to explicitly test for them risks creating insurmountable barriers to deployment, or risks systems being deployed that are not actually safe to use in practice, which will be discussed further below in the section on the ethics of artificial intelligence systems. There is a trade-off between the scientific desire to generate reproducible results in machine learning and artificial intelligence research by standardising on publicly available benchmarks and performance indicators, and the need to develop systems that work in practice in real-life implementation contexts. Through learning to perform well on publicly available, standardised benchmark datasets, there is a risk that performance 'overfits' the specific features of those commonly used datasets. That is, whenever a system learns from a dataset, there is a risk that the system learns too well to predict the features of that particular dataset rather than learning the underlying generalisable regularities that the dataset represents. To guard against this, having different datasets which may differ in ways that are not anticipated is a good test of generalisability for such a system.

Many of the early COVID-19 prediction models included in the systematic review failed to provide transparency into their data sources used in training that would sufficiently allow validation of their risk of bias and harmful outcomes and did not sufficiently report their limitations, biases or potential issues. Even if an artificial intelligence system appears to work, it is essential to validate that the system does not contain unexpected biases in its data inputs or its outputs. For example, there is a very real risk of a system performing better for one population or demographic group than another due to imbalances in the distribution of the data on which the system was trained, and further, for this to be overlooked due to the implicit or explicit biases in those humans who are developing the system. Guarding against inequity is a matter both of verifying the data used in the development of the system and of verifying the system's performance in practice across different sub-groups of the population.

Moreover, transparency around and a detailed understanding of the dataset used in the development of the model can help to guard against errors. One of the errors that was detected in some of the COVID-19 image-based predictive models was that the dataset used for training included an uncorrected colliding variable relating to age: the dataset included images from both children and adults, but given the age distribution of the serious effects of the disease, the adults were much more likely to be suffering from COVID-19 while the children were much more likely to be suffering from pneumonia of other sources. Thus, training a model on such a dataset is likely to show good predictive performance for COVID-19, while in fact, the model has only learned to tell the difference between images of children's lungs vs. those of adults (which is unlikely to be of much clinical utility). There is of course no failsafe way to guard against errors of this type, but it is clearly important to have a deep understanding of the kinds of 'additional' factors that may be co-varying with the variable of interest in the datasets that are being used in the development of the system and to test specifically for differential outputs relating to those. This need suggests a close interdisciplinary partnership between those with the relevant technical expertise and those with the relevant domain expertise is essential for the successful development of systems that will be safely deployable in practice.

POTENTIAL HARMS, TRUST AND THE NEED FOR INTERPRETABILITY

The more widely artificial intelligence systems are deployed in practice, the more it is important to consider the harms that may arise from their use. The above discussion of biases in datasets and algorithms provides an example of one type of harm: artificial systems may operate in unequal ways, working better for one population group than another, or better for one geographical region than another. For example, a problem that has plagued generative image models – models that are able to produce pictures in response to textual prompts – from their inception still occurs in the most recently released models such as DALL-E (2022): the images generated reflect biases in gender with respect to the profession. For example, for a prompt 'nurse' the model generates images only of women, while for 'lawyer' all the images are of men (Arthur Holland Michel [@WriteArthur], 2022). The same problem, although perhaps to a lesser extent after concerted efforts to mitigate against it, affects search results through all the major search engines – and results from the same underlying problem. How can we expect artificial intelligence systems trained on biased datasets to learn unbiased views of the world?

Harms may also arise directly through the failure of such systems if humans are depending on them in complex ways, such as when self-driving cars misinterpret their environmental data in ways that can cause accidents. They may also arise from the inability of such systems to 'know' what they are saying or doing in a wider context. Artificial conversation agents have to be able to guard against directly or indirectly recommending suicide or any other behaviour with a risk of harm to humans.

It may seem as though such examples are far removed from the application of artificial intelligence systems within scientific discovery, but of course, this is not so, insofar as scientific discoveries are relevant for, or are about, humans, they have the potential to be biased and to cause harm. In cases where an artificial intelligence system is part of a decision-making process, a key question that needs to be addressed is who has responsibility for the resulting decision in case something goes wrong? More broadly, the question can be asked if an artificial intelligence system fails and the failure has consequences, for example, if an automated laboratory system fails it may have economic consequences even if humans suffer no direct harms. In such a situation, where an artificial intelligence system fails in a way that causes harms or has costs, who is responsible? How to address questions such as these is the subject of quite extensive regulatory discussions at national and international levels across disciplines.

We have good guidelines and regulations governing other technological innovations, which may indicate the ways in which systems may be used and not used, which limit the liability of the system developer and marketer for errors when the system is used outside of the ways it was intended to be used, and limit the liability of the user if it is used within its intended and marketed applicability domain. But these regulations depend on the system performance and limitations being verifiable within a certain applicability domain. However, for most modern artificial intelligence systems, we lack the means to implement such verifiability for performance in the face of real-world data inputs which may differ in unexpected ways from the data used in training and model development. Moreover, the regulation does not well cover learning systems, since regulation needs commitments to static and testable and certifiable system behaviours, however, the behaviour of adaptive learning systems will change over time.

There is much talk about the need for trust and trustworthiness for artificial intelligence systems. Trust in artificial intelligence systems may be a result of their performance, earned over time and experience in interacting with such a system. On the other hand, time and experience may be a luxury that a system does not have – it may be essential that a system has been determined to be trustworthy in advance of its deployment, that the system be 'certifiable' (Landgrebe, 2022).

In order to support the development of trust, it is often desirable that the behaviour of a system be *interpretable*. The interpretability of an artificially intelligent system can be seen as the transparency of its behaviour with respect to its inputs. Does the system provide reasons or explanations for its behaviour? Can it be determined which aspects of the input were relevant for determining the output? Some model architectures are more interpretable than others. Machine reasoning-based models, based on logic, are fully interpretable in the sense that it is always completely transparent how the inputs determine the outputs. But most highly performant modern artificial intelligence systems are based on deep learning architectures that are not transparent, as the relationship between inputs and outputs is implemented in millions or billions of numeric parameters, and therefore in practice, even if they were transparent they would not be interpretable at all.

All else being equal, the less interpretable models tend to be the more powerful ones, leading to a perceived trade-off between interpretability and performance (Luo *et al.*, 2019), as the more performant systems tend to have more complex inner states which are more difficult to explain (Abdullah, Zahid and Ali, 2021). This has led to a debate between the relative merit and importance of these attributes, with some studies finding that interpretability is more important for trust in, for example, clinical contexts (e.g., Alam and Mueller, 2021), while others have found that accuracy is more important (e.g., van der Veer *et al.*, 2021). However, not all errors are equal (Hutchinson *et al.*, 2022), nor are all explanations equal (Bell *et al.*, 2022; Schoeffer, Kuehl and Machowski, 2022). Moreover, these parameters are not independent. Interpretability indirectly helps support model performance, by helping model developers to diagnose and correct problems during model development, and guard against bias. For example, if it can be determined through interpretability that a model is making the right predictions, but for the wrong reasons, then that is a good indication that the model risks under-performing when it is deployed in a real-world context. Without interpretability, it may not be possible to inspect what the reasons are for the predictions that the model is making. Thus, it may not be possible to diagnose problems before the model is deployed. But with interpretability, the longer-term performance of the system and its fitness for deployment can be more robustly ensured. Moreover, even though some architectures are not intrinsically interpretable in themselves, there are strategies that can be used to add some level of post-hoc interpretability even to those models, by systematically investigating the relationships between the inputs and outputs of the system – in other words, by studying the system's behaviour itself and searching for rules and regularities therein (Gilpin *et al.*, 2019).

Another reason why interpretability matters in particular for the use of artificial intelligence in scientific discovery is that the system might itself participate in a new scientific discovery. The performance of the system may be such as to generate new insights, which contribute back to the body of scientific knowledge. But to fully access and make sense of those insights, requires at least some interpretability. For example, in Narayanaswamy *et al.* (2020), an approach for systematically generating explanations from predictions of an artificial intelligence system is used to generate counterfactuals and hypotheses that can be tested in order to refine the understanding of mechanisms based on image processing. For another example of interpretability in deep learning models, in Glauer *et al.* (2022), the inner state of the model is used to visualise how the model processes the input in order to predict the output, which in this case is predicting the chemical class for a given chemical structure. The model pays attention to the parts of the chemical structure that represent sub-groups within the overall chemical structure of relevance for the predicted chemical class. This visualisation about what parts of the input the model was paying attention to when making predictions of a specific output may help users to trust the predictions and increase overall trust in the performance of the system.

Trust in artificial intelligence systems is influenced by many factors (Jermutus et al., 2022; Schwartz et al., 2022), including the system's perceived accuracy and its ability to explain its outputs. Trust is an aspect of the relationship between the humans who use the system and the system itself. Trust is built through reliability and understanding. We may anticipate that at least for the foreseeable future, few systems will have perfect performance. Understanding the behaviour of a system, including in which contexts or for which inputs it works, and where it doesn't, is essential for building trust in such systems. For systems based on artificial intelligence that have been widely adopted into our daily lives, such as GPS-based navigation support systems, or online searching, we as users have built up a good idea of what the applicability of the system is. We (typically) know more or less which types of roads and situations the navigation system will work well for – and when it is going to fail, for example, when roads have been temporarily redirected due to building works, or when countryside roads are very small. We know which types of searches our search engines are likely to return usable results for, and which not – for example, for common names without distinguishing features. But as users, we don't yet have this level of understanding for newer situations in which artificial intelligence systems are just being deployed. And in such situations, transparency and interpretability help to frame the behaviour of the system, allowing users to gradually become familiar with its limitations and thereby build trust.

To advance our understanding of the trust required for artificial systems, it may be helpful to borrow an analogy from humans.

Research in organisational contexts has identified three primary attributes driving trustworthiness (Mayer, Davis and Schoorman, 1995): benevolence, integrity and ability. Benevolence is the extent to which a person is perceived to want to do good, integrity is the extent to which a person is perceived to be adhering to a set of acceptable principles, and ability is the extent to which a person is believed to possess the skills and competencies needed for their position. In the context of artificial intelligence systems, an analogy for ability might be the accuracy of the system on a variety of relevant performance indicators, which is typically the primary outcome reported in the development and marketing of such systems. And an analogy for benevolence is usually a series of additional metrics that may be reported for such systems, such as that the data they are based on is not biased and that their operations are well-founded, the evaluation of which will be supported by the transparency and interpretability of the system. However, the third attribute – integrity – has been somewhat overlooked in current discussions about trust in artificially intelligent systems.

If integrity in humans is evidenced by their conformance to principles, then in artificially intelligent systems, an analogy for integrity would mean that the errors it makes never violate certain constraints reflecting such principles. For example, a self-driving car should never collide with a pedestrian, a chatbot should never recommend suicide, a prescription medication support tool should never prescribe a lethal dose, etc. Thus, it matters not only how rare an error is (which is the typical information reported in performance metrics used to evaluate artificial intelligence systems) but also what the nature of the error is (the analogy for human principles). Taking integrity seriously for trust will mean that artificially intelligent systems must be able to be verified to operate within rigid boundaries reflecting meaningful constraints on their behaviour – conversations that chatbots can never have, recommendations that decisions support systems can never make, and driving manoeuvres that self-driving cars can never perform. However, most artificial intelligence systems being developed at the moment cannot satisfy such constraints. And this, along with other concerns about the functioning of such systems, directly raises ethical considerations.

ETHICAL CONSIDERATIONS RELATED TO ARTIFICIAL INTELLIGENCE SYSTEMS

Like all other developments in science and technology, artificial intelligence is rightly subject to ethical scrutiny and debate. There are several issues that are raised by this technology for which there are no easy answers. We have discussed above the potential for artificial intelligence systems to cause harm and the need for the regulation of such systems. But are there problems to which artificial intelligence should never be applied? For example, it has been argued to be unethical to try to use artificial intelligence systems in criminal justice, such as to 'predict' criminal activities, or to support hiring decisions, such as pre-filtering CVs (Hagendorff, 2021). Data used for training artificial intelligence systems always has historical biases built in. An automated system may thus act in a way that obscures systemic and historical biases, 'laundering' them in a way that gives them a veneer of newfound respectability. This is dangerous when let loose in deciding the opportunities available for real people in the world. Even if such systems did anything other than amplify prejudice and inequality, the challenge is that when a human makes a bad decision, appeals are possible – holding the person responsible for their decision is possible, in a way that has real consequences in the world – a person can lose their job or social standing for making consistently bad decisions, but when an inanimate device makes the same bad decision, there is a veneer of respectability and a loss of responsibility that can be dangerous.

A further ethical concern with the advance of digitalisation into more and more aspects of human life is the risk of increasing surveillance by ever-present technologies and a loss of privacy. When everything one does is being recorded, how to ensure that it remains private? Moreover, there may be concerns about the ownership of artificial intelligence systems – at present, most large-scale systems are owned by big technological companies, such as Google. There is also a concern about the energy requirements of the training of huge models. The modern state-of-the-art language models with billions of parameters are trained for weeks or months in high-performance computing centres with energy costs that exceed the energy use of whole cities (Strubell, Ganesh and Mccallum, 2019). While efforts are also advancing to reduce the energy use of such systems by improving their efficiency, nevertheless with the increasing scale of adoption and development, the future trajectory is not clear.

Regulation is being advanced to try to mitigate the risks posed by artificial intelligence systems and their implementations. However, the challenge posed in regulating systems that adapt and evolve over time is considerable.

REFERENCES

Abdullah, T., Zahid, M. and Ali, W. (2021) 'A review of interpretable ML in health-care: Taxonomy, applications, challenges, and future directions', *Symmetry*, 13, p. 2439. Available at: https://doi.org/10.3390/sym13122439.

Alam, L. and Mueller, S. (2021) 'Examining the effect of explanation on satisfaction and trust in AI diagnostic systems', *BMC Medical Informatics and Decision Making*, 21(1), p. 178. Available at: https://doi.org/10.1186/s12911-021-01542-6.

Arthur Holland Michel [@WriteArthur] (2022) 'With all the cute, quirky #dalle2 AI images that have been circulating these last few days, I wanted to share some other images* that DALL-E 2 also made that you may not have seen. *Warning: these are quite distressing 1/🧵', *Twitter*. Available at: https://twitter.com/WriteArthur/status/1512429306349248512 (Accessed: 13 July 2022).

Ball, P. and Maxmen, A. (2020) 'The epic battle against coronavirus misinformation and conspiracy theories', *Nature*, 581, pp. 371–374.

Bell, A. et al. (2022) 'It's Just Not That Simple: An Empirical Study of the Accuracy-Explainability Trade-off in Machine Learning for Public Policy', in *2022 ACM Conference on Fairness, Accountability, and Transparency. FAccT '22: 2022 ACM Conference on Fairness, Accountability, and Transparency*, Seoul Republic of Korea: ACM, pp. 248–266. Available at: https://doi.org/10.1145/3531146.3533090.

Botvinik-Nezer, R. (2020) 'Variability in the analysis of a single neuroimaging dataset by many teams', *Nature*, 582, pp. 84–88. Available at: https://doi.org/10.1038/s41586-020-2314-9.

Browne, M. (2018) 'Epistemic divides and ontological confusions: The psychology of vaccine scepticism', *Human Vaccines & Immunotherapeutics*, 14(10), pp. 2540–2542. Available at: https://doi.org/10.1080/21645515.2018.1480244.

Cinelli, M. *et al.* (2021) 'The echo chamber effect on social media', *Proceedings of the National Academy of Sciences*, 118(9), p. e2023301118. Available at: https://doi.org/10.1073/pnas.2023301118.

Gilpin, L.H. *et al.* (2019) 'Explaining explanations: An overview of interpretability of machine learning', *arXiv:1806.00069 [cs, stat]* [Preprint]. Available at: http://arxiv.org/abs/1806.00069 (Accessed: 19 August 2021).

Glauer, M. *et al.* (2022) 'Interpretable ontology extension in chemistry', *Semantic Web Journal* [Preprint]. Available at: https://doi.org/10.5281/ZENODO.6023497.

Hagendorff, T. (2021) 'Blind spots in AI ethics', *AI and Ethics* [Preprint]. Available at: https://doi.org/10.1007/s43681-021-00122-8.

Higginson, A.D. and Munafò, M.R. (2016) 'Current incentives for scientists lead to underpowered studies with erroneous conclusions', *PLoS Biology*, 14(11), p. e2000995. Available at: https://doi.org/10.1371/journal.pbio.2000995.

Hutchinson, B. *et al.* (2022) 'Evaluation Gaps in Machine Learning Practice', in *2022 ACM Conference on Fairness, Accountability, and Transparency. FAccT '22: 2022 ACM Conference on Fairness, Accountability, and Transparency*, Seoul Republic of Korea: ACM, pp. 1859–1876. Available at: https://doi.org/10.1145/3531146.3533233.

Iyengar, S. and Massey, D.S. (2019) 'Scientific communication in a post-truth society', *Proceedings of the National Academy of Sciences*, 116(16), pp. 7656–7661. Available at: https://doi.org/10.1073/pnas.1805868115.

Jermutus, E. *et al.* (2022) 'Influences on user trust in healthcare artificial intelligence: A systematic review', *Wellcome Open Research*. Available at: https://doi.org/10.12688/wellcomeopenres.17550.1.

Juul, J.L. and Ugander, J. (2021) 'Comparing information diffusion mechanisms by matching on cascade size', *Proceedings of the National Academy of Sciences*, 118(46), p. e2100786118. Available at: https://doi.org/10.1073/pnas.2100786118.

Landgrebe, J. (2022) 'Certifiable AI', *Applied Sciences*, 12(3), p. 1050.

Lazer, D.M.J. *et al.* (2018) 'The science of fake news', *Science*, 359(6380), pp. 1094–1096. Available at: https://doi.org/10.1126/science.aao2998.

Luo, Y. *et al.* (2019) 'Balancing accuracy and interpretability of machine learning approaches for radiation treatment outcomes modeling', *BJR Open*, 1(1), p. 20190021. Available at: https://doi.org/10.1259/bjro.20190021.

Mayer, R.C., Davis, J.H. and Schoorman, F.D. (1995) 'An integrative model of organizational trust', *The Academy of Management Review*, 20(3), pp. 709–734. Available at: https://doi.org/10.2307/258792.

Narayanaswamy, A. *et al.* (2020) 'Scientific discovery by generating counterfactuals using image translation', arXiv. Available at: https://doi.org/10.48550/arXiv.2007.05500.

Roberts, M. *et al.* (2021) 'Common pitfalls and recommendations for using machine learning to detect and prognosticate for COVID-19 using chest radiographs and CT scans', *Nature Machine Intelligence*, pp. 1–19. Available at: https://doi.org/10.1038/s42256-021-00307-0.

Roozenbeek, J. and van der Linden, S. (2019) 'Fake news game confers psychological resistance against online misinformation', *Palgrave Communications*, 5(1), p. 65. Available at: https://doi.org/10.1057/s41599-019-0279-9.

Scheufele, D.A. and Krause, N.M. (2019) 'Science audiences, misinformation, and fake news', *Proceedings of the National Academy of Sciences of the United States of America*, 116(16), pp. 7662–7669. Available at: https://doi.org/10.1073/pnas.1805871115.

Schoeffer, J., Kuehl, N. and Machowski, Y. (2022) '"There Is Not Enough Information": On the Effects of Explanations on Perceptions of Informational Fairness and Trustworthiness in Automated Decision-Making', in 2022 ACM Conference on Fairness, Accountability, and Transparency. FAccT '22: 2022 ACM Conference on Fairness, Accountability, and Transparency, Seoul Republic of Korea: ACM, pp. 1616–1628. Available at: https://doi.org/10.1145/3531146.3533218.

Schwartz, J.M. *et al.* (2022) 'Factors influencing clinician trust in predictive clinical decision support systems for in-hospital deterioration: Qualitative descriptive study', *JMIR Human Factors*, 9(2), p. e33960. Available at: https://doi.org/10.2196/33960.

Strubell, E., Ganesh, A. and Mccallum, A. (2019) 'Energy and policy considerations for deep learning in NLP', in Proceedings of the 57th Annual Meeting of the Association for Computational Linguistics, pp. 3645–3650. Available at: https://doi.org/10.18653/v1/P19-1355.

van der Linden, S. *et al.* (2017) 'Inoculating against misinformation', *Science*, 358(6367), pp. 1141–1142. Available at: https://doi.org/10.1126/science.aar4533.

van der Veer, S.N. *et al.* (2021) 'Trading off accuracy and explainability in AI decision-making: Findings from 2 citizens' juries', *Journal of the American Medical Informatics Association*, 28(10), pp. 2128–2138. Available at: https://doi.org/10.1093/jamia/ocab127.

Vosoughi, S., Roy, D. and Aral, S. (2018) 'The spread of true and false news online', *Science*, 359(6380), pp. 1146–1151. Available at: https://doi.org/10.1126/science.aap9559.

Wang, Y. *et al.* (2019) 'Systematic literature review on the spread of health-related misinformation on social media', *Social Science & Medicine* (1982), 240, p. 112552. Available at: https://doi.org/10.1016/j.socscimed.2019.112552.

Wynne, B. (2006) 'public engagement as a means of restoring public trust in science – Hitting the notes, but missing the music?', *Public Health Genomics*, 9(3), pp. 211–220. Available at: https://doi.org/10.1159/000092659.

Yeung, A.W.K. *et al.* (2021) 'Medical and health-related misinformation on social media: Analysis of the scientific literature', *Journal of Medical Internet Research* [Preprint]. Available at: https://doi.org/10.2196/28152.

6

CONCLUSION

AI AND THE FUTURE OF
SCIENTIFIC DISCOVERY

Artificial intelligence technologies are being applied to more and more problems in scientific discovery, and the pace at which these technologies are evolving is currently very rapid. The previous chapters have surveyed some interesting recent developments, but by next year or the year after, we can anticipate these developments will be superseded by even more. A text such as this one can only represent a snapshot at a single moment in time, inevitably losing some of its relevance with the march of progress beyond the point in time at which it was written. To avoid merely reporting on what the current state of the art is, therefore, it is worth taking a longer view across the history of digitalisation in the sciences and the wider context in which current developments are taking place, and even indulging in some speculation about how the current trends might or might not evolve in the near to medium term.

THE FUTURE OF DIGITAL
SCIENTIFIC DISCOVERY

In the early days of the development of artificial intelligence technologies, most of the development was focused on direct, logical encodings of representations of the world and associated automated

DOI: 10.1201/9781003226642-6

logic-based reasoning mechanisms. These led to the early 'expert systems' developed in the 1960s for applications in science and medicine. Early expert systems can be categorised as knowledge-based reasoning systems, and their popularity waned when it became evident that they required huge knowledge bases that were difficult to maintain, that much of the knowledge for real-world applications was not easily captured in a crisp logic-based formalism allowing only statements that were definitively true or false, and that the systems were unable to function if there were any logical contradictions in their knowledge bases. Nevertheless, despite these challenges and the resulting cooling-off of expectations for the applicability of this paradigm of expert systems as a strategy towards autonomous decision-making across scientific disciplines, the technology remained and evolved.

Technologies based on logical representation and inference have led to many of the core technologies that are in daily use for many aspects of digitalisation in science and industry: relational databases, query engines, rules engines, formal semantics for data description, standardisation and exchange, and systems verification. It is rare that such technologies are still described as artificial intelligence, but they are in widespread and pervasive use throughout scientific discovery. This is evidence of one of the curious paradoxes of the development of artificial intelligence technologies – once a particular technological innovation has become established and is therefore no longer mysterious, it tends not to be seen as artificial intelligence anymore. Perhaps, if we do not understand a machine's behaviour, we are more likely to view it as artificially intelligent. But of course, this means that writing a book about artificially intelligent systems is like building a house on shifting sands. Will the artificially intelligent systems of today still be considered artificially intelligent tomorrow?

The present primary focus of developments in artificial intelligence technologies is the paradigm of machine learning from large datasets where the architecture of the system that is learning is built around interconnected layers of 'artificial neurons', each of which represents a function that produces output based on its inputs, with the neurons in subsequent layers depending on neurons in earlier layers, and then the whole system is trained using sophisticated mathematical optimisation strategies. These types of network connectivity-based systems are much better than their logic-based cousins at coping with vagueness and uncertainty in their inputs, and thus they have found many applications for learning from real-world data. They are extremely powerful when sufficient data of sufficient quality can be amassed to train them, as long as the problem they are put towards can be transformed into one that is suitable for being approximated by a quantitative function. And as we have seen in the preceding pages, many problems in scientific discovery can indeed be characterised as such.

In the immediate future, we can expect to see advances in artificial intelligence systems both from better, cleverer architectures and from larger datasets and better datasets being made available for training. There will also be advances that are due to the inventiveness or creativity with which learning and reasoning architectures are applied to solving scientific discovery problems, and advances in the interplay between laboratory automation and the development of intelligent sensing technology and processing of rich input signals.

But as we have also seen, these types of systems have their limits. In the previous chapter, problems of bias and limits in applicability were discussed; others have emphasised inherent limitations in the technology (Landgrebe and Smith, 2022). While it is of course futile to try to predict the future with any level of accuracy, we might speculate – along with others (e.g., Marcus, 2020) – that there will come a time when the most performant artificially intelligent systems are those that are modular and able to harness the best of each different technological family and integrate them together in order to flexibly and adaptively integrate prior knowledge, learning and reasoning and thereby to find relevant information, solve problems, interpret data and address challenges as they arise.

This vision for how intelligent systems might evolve to be more robust in the future is inspired by observations about intelligence in humans, and in particular the apparent modularity of different human cognitive capabilities, and the distinction between rapid-processing but inexact forms of cognition as compared to slower, logically more robust and powerful reasoning capabilities, which distinction Kahnemann famously referred to as 'thinking fast and slow' (Kahneman, 2011). By analogy for artificial intelligence systems, Booch et al. (2020 suggest that we may need different modules which exemplify different types of reasoning also in artificial intelligence: an intuitive, rapid, learned-association type of reasoning as may be exemplified by systems along the lines of modern deep neural networks, alongside slower, more rationally accessible kinds of logical reasoning that are able to rigidly consider all possible constraints and follow detailed chains of inference and reason from logical axioms to conclusions.

At present, advances in artificial intelligence are largely separated between paradigms – advances in sensor-processing and learning technologies are largely separate from advances in logic-based reasoning, and advances in logic-based reasoning are largely separate from advances in other aspects of artificial intelligence, such as causal reasoning (Yao et al., 2020), spatial and temporal reasoning (Zhang et al., 2021), the ability to abstract or generalise by inference to the best hierarchical level for an explanation (Sharp, Fradkin and Eldar, 2022) and even ethical reasoning (Schramowski et al., 2020). The existence of modules with different capabilities suggests a model of artificial intelligence for the future that involves a multi-component system and an agentive 'controller' or governance framework that determines which module is needed and when.

Bringing these different modules together into a system that is able to integrate knowledge and data with learning and reasoning in order to support scientific research will have a far-reaching impact, in particular if such a system is able to access all the knowledge that humans have thus far generated. But the organising principle for the knowledge from which such a system learns will need to be knowledgeable as organised and structured by humans – with human perspectives, and human meanings. And aside from small exceptions, such a digital ecosystem does not yet exist. What would it take to create it?

THE DIGITAL ECOSYSTEM OF DISCOVERY AND KNOWLEDGE

Scientific discovery is a pervasive feature of modern life. So, too, is the advance of digitalisation and the technological progress, including in artificial intelligence technologies, on which it rests. Yet, despite the scale and pace of progress, there is a sense of fragmentation, a sense in which each discovery, each innovation, arises in a silo, in isolation from the other innovations, and too many discoveries and innovations are never fully adopted, never achieve their full impact. There is no single person who is able to consume and process all the innovations and advances in any field, and when viewed across different disciplines, the scale and complexity of the progress are even more staggering – as is the scale and complexity of the challenge of integrating and harnessing these discoveries. At present, within the current paradigm of scientific discovery, it is not possible to know everything that is known, even within a single discipline, nor to access or harness every discovery and innovation. We are collectively wasting resources doing experiments that have already been done or 'losing' the discoveries we have already made, as they become a single grain of sand buried under an impenetrable mountain of similar grains of sand. How could this work differently in the future, with the help of artificial intelligence technologies?

In a vision of how scientific discovery might be in the future, no contribution of relevant scientific findings would ever any longer be lost or overlooked. Comprehensive, systematic, searchable catalogues of the results of scientific research would always be available – captured at source, in digitalised laboratories, and integrated and made searchable by sophisticated algorithms. These catalogues would be very well described and indexed, in ways that are meaningful and detailed, as to the nature of the protocols followed in the research, the subjects, the associated theories and the questions asked, not just what the final results were. Each new discovery would be automatically integrated with the entire body of pre-existing knowledge, adding weight to the interpretations it supports, while still allowing room for theoretical diversity. These catalogues should ideally be able to present their wealth of knowledge in any human natural language, as well as to provide supporting data in summaries and visualisations that help aid understanding. The line between 'encyclopaedic' knowledge and knowledge that is amassed directly at the cutting edge of research will start to blur.

To make this feasible will require currently isolated discovery and knowledge management processes to be integrated into a multi-component ecosystem for discovery science across domains and disciplines. This ecosystem must simultaneously support multiple levels of detail analogous to 'zooming': from a broad overview of all the research on a given topic down to the detailed evidence supporting each finding.

It further needs to be actively learning in the sense that new findings need to rapidly feed into it, which will be possible at scale only if it is built around artificial intelligence technologies that are able to integrate semantic content with powerful machine learning approaches. The ecosystem needs to speak the same languages of science as the humans who create the discoveries and interpret the findings, which means it needs to be built around community-wide shared semantic frameworks and scientific ontologies.

Digitalisation and interconnection of all the components of scientific discovery will be required to create this ecosystem: data, observations, theories, predictions, experimental protocols and robotic experimental assistants, learning technologies, reports, aggregations across studies, narratives and databases. Individually, many of these different components are being digitalised, and tools and protocols which support open science are becoming more commonplace. Scientific ontologies and the artificial intelligence technologies that support data curation, storage, exchange and discovery are already transforming research processes and practices. Knowledge needs to be summarised and accessible at different levels, corresponding to the different educational stages – primary level, secondary, tertiary – and narrative descriptions and theoretical interpretations will allow data to be transparently 'viewed' in different ways, showing rather than hiding how different interpretations and assumptions can potentially change the meaning of the data. This includes disciplinary boundaries. What are the different theoretical foundations for the different disciplinary lenses through which we view and interpret data and how are these foundations related? The history of knowledge and the history of theoretical frameworks are also part of the relevant information that we need to have available, searchable, zoomable and integrated.

Figure 6.1 illustrates interrelationships and flows relating to a given entity or group of entities within the process of scientific discovery, knowledge creation and construction, from experiment through interpretation to publication and media reporting (Hastings, 2021). The use of shared semantic representations – organised around meaningful common entities with clear definitions, managed by communities working together – across these

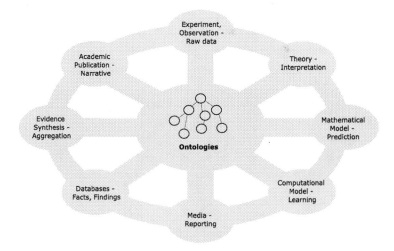

Figure 6.1 An integrated view of the ecosystem of components of scientific discovery.

different aspects allows scientific findings, outcomes and aggregate bodies of evidence to be presented as a whole, consistently against the same shared background. In turn, the adoption of a shared background facilitates a more grounded media presentation, less susceptible to sensationalism. Stabilising the evidence for the accumulation of knowledge via centralisation and exchange allows pockets of uncertainty and contradictions in the evidence base to become more apparent, which paradoxically may serve to increase trust in science overall (van der Bles *et al.*, 2020). It is furthermore important for public trust that the knowledge ecosystem is maintained and managed by a plurality of cooperating public institutions and that a large degree of international cooperation is evident – the risk of bias should be actively managed for all participants. No one institute should dominate, nor one country or language.

There are exciting new developments in technologies for widespread interlinked scientific data and knowledge representation, such as the Open Research Knowledge Graph (Auer, 2018). However, few of the cross-connecting information flows are yet in place. Thus, researchers or consumers wishing to connect different components have a difficult task at present. This is particularly severe for those who need to work on questions that cross multiple topic areas from multiple disciplines, as different discipline-specific approaches may have idiosyncratic infrastructures that may not be easy to apply in combination.

One pressing question is how to bring the scientific research community itself directly and actively into the process of curating its own findings into an aggregated whole. Achieving this will involve more than good intentions: powerful incentives are needed to change embedded practices. Scientists will be more motivated to contribute to shared knowledge resources if those resources enable them to answer scientific questions that would not otherwise be answerable. The movement to address the reproducibility of science as a whole is an important driver for change, in the ongoing dialogue between theory, evidence and discovery (Nosek *et al.*, 2021). To further address fragmentation and in particular, the gaps that develop between different disciplines and theoretical perspectives, theoretical integration and translation within and between disciplines is needed, which requires both explicit formalisation of theories and the mapping of the elements of theories to the elements of ontologies in order to systematically link between theory and evidence (Hastings, Michie and Johnston, 2020). In addition to theoretical integration, it is also important to be able to connect predictive mathematical and computational models using the same layered, meaning-centric ontologies as indexes, and for the systems that interpret novel data to also be theoretically informed (Karpatne et al., 2017). And, for at least the foreseeable future, while the final say about data interpretation, theoretical advances and the meaning of scientific discovery are still made by humans, the tools that support and partially automate the process of interfacing between human meanings and digital meanings will need to be embedded deeply into every scientific workflow, reducing the burden associated with keeping clean and usable data and metadata.

Thus, we see that digital transformation and the availability of artificial intelligence technologies support scientific discovery but they also need to support scientists and the processes of scientific research, as well as make the outputs of such research more coherently navigable, in a far-reaching methodological shift that has the potential to bring about a new unification within and between bodies of knowledge and practice and radically speed up the discovery process.

On this point, it is worth coming back to the question of what artificial intelligence is. If we frame the answer to this question as only the possibility of machines being able to do the things that humans can do, we risk missing the greatest opportunity of all for these technologies: that they can do *different* things to what humans can do. In many ways, although it is understandably exciting if we are able to develop artificial systems that are able to do things that humans can do, what we need the most are systems that are able to do things that humans cannot do, such as 'reading' thousands of new research papers every day, managing thousands of repetitive mini-experiments in a laboratory every day, and hunting for patterns in thousands of data points. This suggests systems being developed in such a way that machines and humans can work in partnership, in hybrids of human intelligence and machine intelligence (Wiethof and Bittner, 2021), which may, in time, paradoxically, allow humans to become more human again (Israni and Verghese, 2019).

THE FUTURE OF ARTIFICIAL INTELLIGENCE FOR SCIENTIFIC DISCOVERY

Just as artificial intelligence is driving forward scientific discovery, and has the potential to do so even more in the future, scientific discovery has been and continues to be a driver for pushing forward the frontier of artificial intelligence. The current paradigm of large-scale learning from huge datasets has achieved many successes, but to make even further advances, different paradigms are needed. One such paradigm shift is towards the development of algorithms that can harness pre-existing knowledge in order to perform well in situations in which there are fewer and more heterogeneous datasets available for data-driven learning. Explicit representations of knowledge and theoretical tenets may reduce the quantities of data required for learning by making the learning approach better informed (von Rueden *et al.*, 2021), and focused more on deeper meanings. The current generation of large language models, with billions of parameters, trained to predict the next words in sentences, are not learning meaning (Lake and Murphy, 2021) – they are not learning to understand the text that they are so adept at predicting (Bender and Koller, 2020). They tend to learn statistical features of their data input spaces without learning the generalisable principles behind those texts (Zhang *et al.*, 2022). Meaning involves the relationship between what is communicated (form) and what is intended to be communicated (communicative intent), and the latter necessarily involves a generalised representation of the world in some way, not just the structure of language, which is all that language models have to learn from. Meaning understanding is tested by more difficult exercises than are usually posed to language models, questions that probe understanding and generalisation to novel situations, rather than just form and superficial interactivity (Santoro *et al.*, 2021).

Another way in which scientific discovery has the potential to benefit artificial intelligence is through advances in the science of human intelligence, in the understanding of the brain, the mind and behaviour. Even though the artificial intelligence algorithms of the current generation – those for machine learning, and those for machine reasoning – are inspired by human intelligence to some extent, they draw only from small fragments of the overall understanding of the brain and the mind that has been developing over the last decades (Heaven, 2021). There are several important dimensions in human intelligence that have thus far been overlooked in the development of artificial intelligence. The first is that human intelligence, and human learning, is embodied and has evolved as a capability to act intelligently in the environment (Sternberg, 2019, 2021). Babies learn by exploring and interacting with their worlds. That is how they test their understanding of what they perceive, and how they develop an implicit understanding of causality. Can we expect artificially intelligent systems to be able to learn about the world without being able to interact with the world as a part of their individual learning processes?

In this aspect, advances in artificial intelligence algorithms may come from advances in the design of automated robotic agents. The second is that human intelligence is intrinsically multi-modal – we garner sensory inputs from multiple different sensory input modalities at the same time, such as touch, vision, and hearing. These convergent input streams which are about the same underlying reality – a reality which in turn we are able to interact with – allow us to build confidence in our correct understanding of the world. Without cross-anchoring our understanding across different inputs, it would be much harder to be sure that we had developed a good, predictive understanding of how the world works, the foundation of intelligent action. To address this, research needs to focus on predictive learning across multiple convergent modalities (Fei et al., 2022; Holzinger et al., 2022). Finally, humans develop their intelligence via continuous learning over time, adding nuance and complexity without forgetting what has already been learned before. This type of continuous learning from ongoing observations, additional training and interactions requires that artificial intelligence systems maintain state over long periods of time while undergoing additional training and improvement in performance. To this end research in artificial intelligence needs to develop techniques for continuous learning from sparse examples that more closely parallel and are informed by studies of learning in humans (Kim et al., 2020), and to work towards artificial intelligence systems that are aware of their own levels of knowledge (Osband et al., 2022).

The role of artificial intelligence in science in the future might not just be to support discovery but to advance scientific *understanding* (Krenn et al., 2022) by serving (a) as a computational 'microscope', providing information not yet attainable by experiments by a new synergy between measurement, prediction and simulation, that allows more detailed time and spatial scales to be probed than can be measured at present, (b) as a resource of inspiration, an 'artificial muse', expanding the scope of human imagination and creativity and (c) to be an agent of scientific *understanding*, by supporting processes that generalise from observations and transfer scientific concepts and theories to new phenomena. To achieve this vision will involve continual co-evolution between science itself and the algorithms and technologies that support and drive science forward, between the sciences of human intelligence and the intelligence involved in the creation of artificial intelligence. It will involve increasing permeability across previous disciplinary boundaries, and the alignment of artificial systems with the wider context of the values, ethics and processes involved in scientific research within human societies (Koster et al., 2022).

It is the nature of discovery that we cross the border between what is known and what is not known, what is possible and what is not possible. Scientific discovery is a process that feeds on itself, that sometimes appears to be accumulating foundations that have no architecture, like shifting sands, but which suddenly solidify into a tower from which it is possible to see further than ever before. Technological development, such as that of artificial intelligence technology, advances side by side with scientific discovery, growing together with it, feeding on it, and in turn contributing to it, at times in ways that are predictable, and at other times in ways that sweep aside what is ordinary and utterly transform the horizon of what is possible. At a time in the history of the planet when it can seem as though crisis after crisis is blasting at the foundations of the world as we know it, digital and societal transformation may seem frightening or desperately necessary, alternatively the stuff of nightmares or dreams, but in such moments it is worth remembering that transformation is not something that happens to us but that we build, that we create in our endless cumulative efforts to solve problems, answer questions, construct useful tools, and probe ever deeper into the mysteries of reality.

REFERENCES

Auer, S. (2018) *Towards an open research knowledge graph*, Zenodo. Available at: https://doi.org/10.5281/zenodo.1157185.

Bender, E.M. and Koller, A. (2020) 'Climbing towards NLU: On Meaning, Form, and Understanding in the Age of Data', in *Proceedings of the 58th Annual Meeting of the Association for Computational Linguistics. Proceedings of the 58th Annual Meeting of the Association for Computational Linguistics*, Online: Association for Computational Linguistics, pp. 5185–5198. Available at: https://doi.org/10.18653/v1/2020.acl-main.463.

Booch, G. *et al.* (2020) 'Thinking fast and slow in AI', *arXiv:2010.06002* [*cs*] [Preprint]. Available at: http://arxiv.org/abs/2010.06002 (Accessed: 10 January 2022).

Fei, N. *et al.* (2022) 'Towards artificial general intelligence via a multimodal foundation model', *Nature Communications*, 13(1), p. 3094. Available at: https://doi.org/10.1038/s41467-022-30761-2.

Hastings, J. (2021) 'Scientific ontologies, digital curation and the learning knowledge ecosystem', *Qurator, CEUR Workshop Proceedings*, 2836, p. 9.

Hastings, J., Michie, S. and Johnston, M. (2020) 'Theory and ontology in behavioural science', *Nature Human Behaviour*, 4(3), pp. 226–226. Available at: https://doi.org/10.1038/s41562-020-0826-9.

Heaven, W.D. (2021) 'We'll never have true AI without first understanding the brain', MIT Technology Review. Available at: https://www.technologyreview.com/2021/03/03/1020247/artificial-intelligence-brain-neuroscience-jeff-hawkins/ (Accessed: 18 July 2022).

Holzinger, A. *et al.* (2022) 'Information fusion as an integrative cross-cutting enabler to achieve robust, explainable, and trustworthy medical artificial intelligence', *Information Fusion*, 79, pp. 263–278. Available at: https://doi.org/10.1016/j.inffus.2021.10.007.

Israni, S.T. and Verghese, A. (2019) 'Humanizing artificial intelligence', *JAMA*, 321(1), pp. 29–30. Available at: https://doi.org/10.1001/jama.2018.19398.

Kahneman, D. (2011) *Thinking, Fast and Slow.* New York, NY: Farrar, Straus and Giroux.

Karpatne, A. *et al.* (2017) 'Theory-guided data science: A new paradigm for scientific discovery from data', *IEEE Transactions on Knowledge and Data Engineering*, 29(10), pp. 2318–2331. Available at: https://doi.org/10.1109/TKDE.2017.2720168.

Kim, D. *et al.* (2020) 'On the reliability and generalizability of brain-inspired reinforcement learning algorithms'. Available at: https://doi.org/10.48550/arXiv.2007.04578.

Koster, R. *et al.* (2022) 'Human-centred mechanism design with democratic AI', *Nature Human Behaviour*, pp. 1–10. Available at: https://doi.org/10.1038/s41562-022-01383-x.

Krenn, M. *et al.* (2022) 'On scientific understanding with artificial intelligence', *arXiv:2204.01467 [physics]* [Preprint]. Available at: http://arxiv.org/abs/2204.01467 (Accessed: 5 April 2022).

Lake, B.M. and Murphy, G.L. (2021) 'Word meaning in minds and machines', *arXiv:2008.01766 [cs]* [Preprint]. Available at: http://arxiv.org/abs/2008.01766 (Accessed: 16 August 2021).

Landgrebe, J. and Smith, B. (2022) *Why Machines Will Never Rule the Earth: AI Without Fear.* New York, NY: Routledge.

Marcus, G. (2020) 'The next decade in AI: Four steps towards robust artificial intelligence', *arXiv:2002.06177 [cs]* [Preprint]. Available at: http://arxiv.org/abs/2002.06177 (Accessed: 5 September 2021).

Nosek, B.A. *et al.* (2021) *Replicability, robustness, and reproducibility in psychological science*, PsyArXiv. Available at: https://doi.org/10.31234/osf.io/ksfvq.

Osband, I. *et al.* (2022) 'Epistemic neural networks'. arXiv. Available at: http://arxiv.org/abs/2107.08924 (Accessed: 18 July 2022).

Santoro, A. *et al.* (2021) 'Symbolic behaviour in artificial intelligence', *arXiv:2102.03406 [cs]* [Preprint]. Available at: http://arxiv.org/abs/2102.03406 (Accessed: 6 May 2021).

Schramowski, P. *et al.* (2020) 'The moral choice machine', *Frontiers in Artificial Intelligence*, 3. Available at: https://www.frontiersin.org/articles/10.3389/frai.2020.00036 (Accessed: 16 July 2022).

Sharp, P.B., Fradkin, I. and Eldar, E. (2022) 'Hierarchical inference as a source of human biases', *Cognitive, Affective, & Behavioral Neuroscience* [Preprint]. Available at: https://doi.org/10.3758/s13415-022-01020-0.

Sternberg, R.J. (2019) 'A theory of adaptive intelligence and its relation to general intelligence', *Journal of Intelligence*, 7(4), p. E23. Available at: https://doi.org/10.3390/jintelligence7040023.

Sternberg, R.J. (2021) 'Adaptive intelligence: intelligence is not a personal trait but rather a person × task × situation interaction', *Journal of Intelligence*, 9(4), p. 58. Available at: https://doi.org/10.3390/jintelligence9040058.

van der Bles, A.M. *et al.* (2020) 'The effects of communicating uncertainty on public trust in facts and numbers', *Proceedings of the National Academy of Sciences*, 117(14), pp. 7672–7683. Available at: https://doi.org/10.1073/pnas.1913678117.

von Rueden, L. *et al.* (2021) 'Informed machine learning - A taxonomy and survey of integrating prior knowledge into learning systems', *IEEE Transactions on Knowledge and Data Engineering*, pp. 1–1. Available at: https://doi.org/10.1109/TKDE.2021.3079836.

Wiethof, C. and Bittner, E. (2021) 'Hybrid intelligence - Combining the human in the loop with the computer in the loop: A systematic literature review', in Proceedings of the International Conference on Information Systems (ICIS 2021), Austin, Texas, USA.

Yao, L. *et al.* (2020) 'A survey on causal inference', arXiv. Available at: https://doi.org/10.48550/arXiv.2002.02770.

Zhang, C. *et al.* (2021) 'Abstract spatial-temporal reasoning via probabilistic abduction and execution', arXiv. Available at: https://doi.org/10.48550/arXiv.2103.14230.

Zhang, H. *et al.* (2022) 'On the paradox of learning to reason from data', arXiv. Available at: https://doi.org/10.48550/arXiv.2205.11502.

INDEX

Printed in the United States
by Baker & Taylor Publisher Services